The Battling Bells
and Fighting Flemings

Marti Bennett

The Battling Bells and Fighting Flemings

A tribute to our earliest Bell ancestor, Robert Bell and Agnes Fleming Bell, and the proud Scots Irish heritage they passed on to their future generations. In many ways each of us is the sum total of what our ancestors were. The virtues they had may be our virtues, their strengths our strengths, and in a way their challenges could be our challenges. This book is an attempt to portray why our ancestors left Scotland for northern Ireland, and eventually from Europe to travel across the Atlantic to America. May we draw strength, inspiration, and wisdom from the conditions, battles, condemnations, and even discriminations our ancestors faced in their daily lives.

Beautiful Scottish Thistle - A National Emblem

Unfortunately for those unwary Viking invaders, one of their soldiers bare feet came down hard on a Scottish thistle and his cries of shock and pain were enough to wake the sleeping Scots. Leaping to their feet, the clansmen charged into battle and the rest, as they say, is history... and yes, the fiery Scots were victorious! Legend has it that because of the heroic role the plant played in the outcome of the battle, the thistle was immediately chosen as a national emblem. Now, how much of this is truth no-one knows, but we do know that by the 15th century the Scottish thistle was being used as a national emblem.

Today the Thistle is seen on everything from sporrans and jewelry to soap and tea-towels. It's a Scottish symbol recognized all over the world. That little weed has come a long way! This biennial plant (which means it takes two years to complete its life-cycle) is also known as the 'Cotton Thistle', and its Latin name is 'Onopordum Acanthium' . The 'basic' growth of leaves, roots and stems happens during the first year, the plant flowers during the second year, and then it dies. Luckily, these types of plants reseed easily and new plants will spring up around the original every year. In fact, anyone who's actually encountered the Thistle will tell you that it 'grows like a weed', and that's the truth! During its second year, this Thistle can grow up to eight feet in height, and over four feet in width. When you realize that, in spite of the soft downy flowers, the bulk of this plant is covered in extremely sharp thorns, you can imagine just how impressive (and dangerous) it can be. If you've ever stepped on a thistle, you'll have some sympathy for the poor

Vikings in the legend above. This plant also has a very stubborn and invasive root system, and removing the entire plant from a piece of ground is not an easy task. If you miss just a little bit of the root, you'll find the thistles come back in force the following year.

So why would a population choose a weed as its symbol? A closer look at the story of Scotland may give us a clue. To quote Nigel Tranter, in his *History of Scotland, the Scottish people have a real story to tell..."folks who lived and died, loved and hated, fought and suffered, laughed and wept, and in doing so grew into a nation, a great nation which, small in numbers, is accepted the world over as amongst the foremost in character and achievement...and folly! The Scots are a very odd people and have always been, a sort of animated contradiction in terms, capable of higher heights and lower depths than most; courageous, adventurous, intemperate, disputations, romantic – however much they may disclaim it – sentimental, religious in the widest sense, and much more."*

After reading the stories and tales of our courageous ancestors, we may also think that this plant is the perfect Scottish Emblem! May we Scots Irish descendants take inspiration from our Bell/Fleming ancestors, and the strength to face our own battles.This book is an attempt to follow our Bell trail, starting with Robert and Agnes Fleming Bell. Emigrating from Ireland in the mid-1740's, this trail fans out to Virginia, and eventually to the Western Pennsylvania counties of Westmoreland, Allegheny, Indiana, and Jefferson. The Scottish naming pattern makes genealogy research more challenging! We know our Bells came from Scotland, the difficulty/challenge is discovering from which of the many Bell Clans we descend. As DNA testing becomes more widespread and detailed, the genes may indeed provide the Clan answers we are seeking.

As with many other people living in Western PA, we share Irish diaspora heritage. The Government of Ireland defines the Irish diaspora as "all persons of Irish nationality, who habitually reside outside of the island of Ireland." In researching this book, it struck me how similar the challenges are between our immigrant ancestors and today's immigrants, trying to seek asylum in our southern states. Many of us, who can actually remember our world history days, learned about the social classes in the Feudal age. We were taught you were basically born into the social class where you would remain all your life. The lowest social level were the peasants – and it was from this class that came virtually all Scots, whose descendants became Scots Irish. To our ears, the word "peasant" has a prejudicial sound, with connotations of dullness, even stupidity. At least they didn't use the terms rapists, murders, drug addicts, pests, illegal aliens, animals, etc, like our present POTUS likes to throw out. In European usage, the term peasant means simply a tiller of the soil, who, in the natural order of things, lacked the privileges and responsibilities of the gentry and nobility. A peasant may indeed be dull and unwilling to change because of tradition or a fixed opinion, but he or she might also be thrifty and ambitious, a real force in their community.

This book is dedicated to my uncle, Robert Bell Pierce, and all my first cousins and their descendants on the Bell line.

Bell Name Meaning

Scottish and northern English: from Middle English belle 'bell', in various applications; most probably an occupational name for a bell ringer or bell maker, or a topographic name for someone living 'at the bell' (as attested by 14th-century forms such as John atte Belle). This indicates either residence by an actual bell (e.g. a town's bell in a bell tower, centrally placed to summon meetings, sound the alarm, etc.) or 'at the sign of the bell', i.e. a house or inn sign (although surnames derived from house and inn signs are rare in Scots and English). Scottish and northern English: from the medieval personal name Bel. As a man's name this is from Old French beu, bel 'handsome', which was also used as a nickname. As a female name it represents a short form of Isobel, a form of Elizabeth.

Who Do You Think You Are?

Connections to Our Bell Ancestry and Scots Irish Heritage

Edna Todd Bell is our major link to the proud Scots-Irish heritage that comprises much of the early history of America. Other roots, including the Pierce, Bennett, Manson, Shea, and Bowman lines, also include Scots-Irish links, but for the purposes of this book, the focus is on the Bells.

1905 High School Senior Picture

1915 Engagement Picture

Edna Todd Bell, born in 1890, is the eldest child of a Scots-Irish father, and Scots-Irish/German mother. Her father, whose early careers included teacher, administrator, and lawyer, raised his two children by himself after his wife passed away in 1904. In frail health himself, John Taylor Bell was forced to turn away from the rigors of education and courtroom, and instead took his talents in a slightly different direction – selling encyclopedias and text books. He still maintained contact with the education process though - being elected to the Indiana School Board, eventually being selected President. Since the family house was located in the borough of Indiana, Edna would have attended the Second Ward School, located in what is now the middle of 5th Street. That school was demolished when the present-day Horace Mann School was built in 1908-1909. Edna took over the mothering role, basically raising her brother, Hugh Todd Bell, who was five years younger. Graduating from Indiana High School in 1905, Edna delayed her college education until Todd graduated from high school.

14   HOLLINS COLLEGE

Academic Honors

Session 1914-1915

Bachelors of Arts

ANGIER, MARY ESTELLE.................................Illinois
BELL, EDNA TODD...................................Pennsylvania
BOSWELL, MARGARET LEE............................Virginia
CAMP, ELIZABETH BRETT.............................Florida
HEARSEY, MARGUERITE CAPEN....................New Jersey
MARTIN, BESSIE TAYLOR.........................West Virginia
MUSE, WILLIE HOWARD.................................Georgia
STEARNES, MAY CONSTANCE.........................Virginia
WARD, AILEEN...................................South Carolina
WATKINS, MELLE....................................Louisiana
WATSON, MARTHA EDWARDS..................South Carolina

The President's Medal for Scholarship

EDNA TODD BELL of Pennsylvania.

According to her son, Bob, she enrolled in Indiana Normal School, now known as IUP, for a year, then transferred to Hollins College in 1911. Hollins College is located in Roanoke, VA, an all-women's college founded in 1842. Immersing herself in college life, Edna quickly made her mark, being nominated and elected one of the Associates to both the monthly *The Hollins Magazine* and

The Spinster, a newsletter which was published near the end of semesters. This was no small matter, as these Associates were elected by a board of editors, selected from the College literary societies, as well as elected by the student body. According to what college records were available, I was able to discover Edna majored in history, graduated in three years, and was the recipient of several academic awards, including the prestigious Presidential Medal for Scholarship. She was also awarded an award for Proficiency in Psychology and Ethics. Perhaps that was what had her one step ahead of me when it came to reading my mind when trying to escape trouble in my younger days. She always seemed to know who was the guilty grandchild (was creative thinking a sign of intelligence?), who let bullfrogs loose in her kitchen, or put pet white mice in her bed. According to her son, Edna was fluent in both Latin and Greek. I can assure you that there is no genetic disposition toward either of those languages in my DNA. None of us thought to ask our grandmother why she chose a college in Virginia to finish her degree, rather than the nearby Indiana Normal School, but the answer may be found in our earliest Bell ancestor in this country. Robert Bell, as well as many other Bells, traveled south from Philadelphia along the Cumberland Wagon Trail. That trail is basically what the present highway, Route 81 follows today. Roanoke is located just off that highway...is it possible there were Bell relatives from the original Bell brother located in the vicinity? DNA results have linked Scotland's Sir Robert Bell, to Bells in the Eastern Shore area of Virginia. Or was it because her brother fled the nest, and enrolled in Michigan State? Perhaps Edna also felt the need to escape the nest, and headed off in a new direction?

Edna was hired to teach in the Indiana Schools until when, at age 26, she met and married a young attorney, William Elliott Pierce in 1917. At the point of choosing marriage and the eventual family rearing, women were forced to resign from teaching. There was no such thing as maternity leave in those days. A woman's perceived sole purpose in life was reproduction, but it was apparent a pregnant woman should crawl under a rock while they were in that condition. It was unthinkable that an obviously-pregnant woman should continue teaching. Heaven-forbid the eyes of the inquisitive children should see the changes a woman goes through during pregnancy. In addition, once married, a female became the property of her husband, and as such, could not receive a paycheck, or even open her own bank account. The years leading up to the passage of the 19th Amendment in 1920 were often filled with turmoil, bizarre statements, and outright lies. There was even an organization, NAOWS – National Association OPPOSED to Woman Suffrage, "formed to oppose women's right to vote, calling it the "petticoat rule." A pamphlet was circulated with NAOWS household cleaning tips, and other gems including: "You do not need a ballot to clean out your sink drain; 90% of the women either do not want the right to vote, or do not care; Because 80% of the women eligible to vote are married and thus can only double or annul their husband's votes; This right means competition of women with men instead of cooperation." And perhaps the most befitting statement "There is no known method for cleansing mud-stained reputations after bitter political campaigns." Thank goodness they didn't have email, Facebook, or Twitter back then!

After 1920, Edna continued to influence the youth of Indiana through substitute teaching and her church. Edna's Scots-Irish ancestors have a long military history, dating back to Robert deBruce of Braveheart fame, while her husband served in the border conflict with Mexico and in both World Wars. Desiring to carry on the military tradition, Edna joined the American Red Cross prior to WWII. She served on the first Indiana County early detection system to warn the area, particularly Pittsburgh, of incoming German planes. Those brave volunteers would sign up to station themselves in the loft of John Campbell's farm, located on the outskirts of Indiana. Any sight of a German plane would result in a phone call to trigger a blackout of the entire region. With today's technology, this seems rather preposterous, but in conversations with my grandmother before her passing, she was justly proud of her contributions. The Military Science Building, on the campus of IUP, is dedicated to her husband, Wm. E. Pierce. The original idea for naming the building was to name it after Edna. True to her unselfish nature, she insisted they name it after her husband. After reading the histories of the battle-hardened Bells and Flemings, we all can take pride in their military history and sense of duty to family and country. Our Scots-Irish story is one of progress from something near barbarism in 1600 to civilization, from ignorance to a passion for education, from backwardness in most fields to daring achievement, from static traditionalism to dynamic individualism – and all of this in the span of four centuries.

Edna Todd Bell and daughter, Martha Elizabeth Pierce - aka Betty Pierce

        Martha (Betty) was born in 1918 at the onset of the Spanish Flu Pandemic.
Both mother and daughter escaped the deadly disease that claimed 50 million,
worldwide. That strain of H1N1 flu virus has made a comeback in recent years, but
modern medicines have proved better than the 1918 treatment of "painting"
infected throats with castor oil and sending the infectious persons back to their
homes. Edna went on to birth three more children, all boys, so Betty found herself
babysitting her two younger brothers. Her father, Colonel William E. Pierce, an
Indiana attorney and WW1 vet, found time to share his passion for golf with his
daughter. Girls sports in high school was unheard of, but the local Indiana Country
Club held tournaments for both women and men. Betty went on to win the coveted
yearly club championship five times. An excellent student, Betty would work
summers filing papers for her father in his law office. When it came time to decide
on a career, the LPGA (Ladies Professional Golf Association) wasn't formed until
1950, so Betty followed in her father's footsteps, settling on the pre-law program at
Duke University in Durham, NC. Her summer experiences spent in her father's
law office certainly didn't hurt her job resume. Brother Bill, three years younger,
also followed in the family footsteps. The first family financial crisis came when
Betty was entering her senior year. Brother Bill had been accepted in the pre-law
program at Allegheny College. Considering the Great Depression was finally over
in 1939, the family could not afford the tuitions to both Duke and Allegheny.
Rather than force her brother to wait a year to enter Allegheny, Betty volunteered
to live at home and finish up her senior year at IUP. Duke honored the IUP classes,
and Betty received her A.B. degree from Duke.

Looming large on the horizon was World War Two. Father William E. would go back in service as an Adjutant, while Mother Edna served with the Indiana Red Cross. Daughter Betty volunteered with the Red Cross and was trained in their Motor Pool Division, which included blackout training. Son William T. graduated from Allegheny, and enlisted in the United States Navy.

On the National level, in May 1941 with war looming, U.S. Rep. Edith Nourse Rogers of Massachusetts introduced a bill for the creation of the Women's Army Auxiliary Corps. Having been a witness to the status of women in World War I, Rogers vowed that if American women served in support of the Army, they would do so with all the rights and benefits afforded to Soldiers. Spurred on by the

December 7, 1941 attack on Pearl Harbor, Congress approved the creation of WAAC on May 14, 1942. President Franklin D. Roosevelt signed the bill into law on May 15, and on May 16, Oveta Culp Hobby was sworn in as the first director. WAAC was established "for the purpose of making available to the national defense the knowledge, skill, and special training of women of the nation."

WAAC Recruitment Poster

  The first WAAC training center was established at Fort Des Moines, Iowa. Anxious to serve, nearly 35,000 women applied for 1,000 open spots. One of those was Betty Pierce. The local newspaper article on her enlistment stated Betty wanted to "do her bit… and I'm a terrible knitter." Applicants were required to be US citizens, between the ages of 21-45 without dependents, at least 5 feet tall, and weighing a minimum of 100 lbs. Her application listed her at 5'4" 115 lbs, age 24. Accepted as one of only 500 women officer applicants nationwide, when Betty entered on 23 July 1942, she was commissioned a 1st Lieutenant.

WAACs were an auxiliary of the Army, meaning they would receive living quarters, uniforms, pay, and food, but would not receive overseas pay, life insurance, and death benefits. WAACs immediately set about training to free up positions held by male soldiers, enabling them to go overseas and fight.

After basic training, Betty was selected for a "special project,' whereby she would be sent to New Orleans as part of a transportation unit. She would be put in charge of a unit of men in the transportation unit. The idea wasn't to see if she could run heavy machinery, as she told me later in life, it was to see if she could lead men. Having three younger brothers, plus her experience in the Indiana County Red Cross Motor Pool, she would have "aced" that test. At that point, Betty was sent to Stanford University's Army Communications and Intelligence School, where she was taught Japanese.

When the war came to a close, most WACs returned home, although a few stayed as part of the occupying force. Betty Pierce was one of the occupying force sent to Japan. After the Japanese surrendered, Betty arrived with the U.S. Army Civil Affairs Detachment. She worked in the Tokyo Post Office with Army Intelligence Censorship. According to her stories, she censored the mail coming in and out of the post office.

Brother Bill enlisted in the Navy on September 9, 1943 in their newly
redesigned naval aviation program. Bill was sent to the Naval Aviation Preparatory

School in Philadelphia. The Naval Aviator Program was created in 1935. Candidates had to be between the ages of 19 to 25, and have at least two years of college. Training was a mandatory 18 months and candidates had to agree to not marry during training, plus serve for at least three more years of active duty service. The Philadelphia school was a "boot camp" course in physical training (to get the cadets in shape and weed out the unfit), military skills (marching, standing in formation, and performing the manual of arms), and naval customs and etiquette. Pre-flight school was a refresher course in mathematics and physics with practical applications of these skills in flight. This was followed by a short preliminary flight training module in which the cadets did 10 hours in a flight simulator, followed by a one-hour flight with an instructor. Those who passed, including William T. Pierce, received their V-5 flight badges (gold-metal aviator wings with the V-5 badge set in the center). They were sent on to primary and basic flight training at the Naval Aviator School at Pensacola, FL. Training for war time missions in Florida involved creative practicing. His daughter related stories from her dad where he recalled flying practice missions along the Florida Gulf coast beaches. Fortunately, WW II ended before Bill was actually sent into combat. He was discharged as an Aviation Cadet Ensign on November 19, 1945, which was considered senior to the rank of chief petty officer, but below the rank of warrant officer.

Bill returned to civilian life and resumed his goal of attending law school. His choice of law schools was Dickinson College in Carlisle, PA. - the same Dickinson College chosen by Alexander Wilson Taylor over 100 years earlier. Coincidence? Maybe, but see my hypothesis later in this book on the source of the Taylor middle name in several generations of our Bell lines.

After being discharged, Betty also returned home to face one of those "crossroads of life" decisions. With age 30 staring her in the face, she could either resume her law career by entering law school, or marry and start a family. Marriage won out, which closed out her law and military career. She did volunteer work at elections, and went door-to-door for the ten year Federal Census records. Her Army days training would periodically resurface in the form of her Girl Scout troops marching in local parades...and I have memories/nightmares of making "military corners" on my bed, and Captain Pierce - now Bennett testing my work with a coin! Fitted sheets would have saved me much frustration, but they were invented long after my childhood days.

More than 150,000 WACs served during WWII and their contributions changed the tides of history. Both Betty and Bill's sense of duty and willingness to step up and accept a challenge is yet another chapter in the Battling Bells and Fighting Flemings book. Those ancestors would be proudly saluting their sense of duty and service.

Captain Martha E. Pierce

Insignia for the WAAC & WAC Uniform

The Heraldic Section was asked to design insignia for collar, lapel and cap, as well as for buttons. Because of metal shortages, olive drab, plastic buttons were specified. The cap insignia was also to be in plastic (later changed to a gold metal). From pencil sketches produced by the Heraldic Section, Director Hobby had a jeweler in New York make, in gold for her own use, a cap insignia of an eagle. This hand-cut eagle proved to be somewhat lopsided but was the design chosen by WAAC Headquarters nonetheless. The WAAC eagle (later dubbed the "buzzard") thus became the design for the hat insignia and the buttons. Officers wore a cut-out insignia on their cap while enlisted women wore the same design superimposed on a disc. The lapel insignia for the WAAC uniform was the head and helmet of the Greek goddess, Pallas Athene, chosen as most symbolic of the WAAC role. A sleeve patch or tab was designed to be worn directly beneath the chevrons. The tab was designed with the letters "WAAC" in moss-toned embroidered on an old-gold background, the WAAC colors.

WW2 Pierce Vets

Edna and William E. Pierce
Martha E. and William T. Pierce

Understanding the History of Great Britain

Before we can examine the DNA results from my uncles, Edward M. and Robert B. Pierce, and the more recent history our known ancestors experienced, we should become familiar with the eon of years that have led up to the most recent six centuries. First, present-day Great Britain is primarily comprised of England, Scotland, Wales, and the northern portion of Ireland. Historically, in Europe, Great Britain also included portions of France, Germany, Denmark, Belgium, Netherlands, Switzerland, Austria, and Italy. In prehistoric Britain, 12,000 years ago at the end of the Last Glacial Age, the sea levels around northern Europe were low enough for Stone Age hunter-gatherers to cross, on foot, into what are now the islands around Great Britain. Farming spread to the islands by about 4000 B.C., and the Neolithic inhabitants constructed their remarkable and puzzling stone monuments, including the famed Stonehenge.

Beginning in about 2500 B.C., successive waves of tribes settled in the region. These tribes are often called "Celts," however that term is an 18th century invention. The Celts were not a nation in any sense, but a widespread group of tribes that shared a common cultural and linguistic background. Originating in central Europe, they spread to dominate most of Western Europe, the British Isles, and the Iberian Peninsula. They even settled as far away as Anatolia, in modern-day Turkey. However, this Celtic dominance could not withstand the rise of the Roman Empire.

After defeating the Celts of Gaul (modern-day France, Luxembourg, Belgium, and western areas of Germany and Switzerland), the Romans invaded the British Isles in 43 A.D. Most of southern Britain was conquered and occupied over the course of a few decades, and became the Roman province of Britannia. Hadrian's Wall, in the north of England, marked the approximate extent of Roman control. Those tribes, who were not assimilated into the Roman Empire, were forced to retreat to other areas that remained Celtic, such as Wales, Ireland, Scotland, the Isle of Man, and Brittany. The Roman presence largely wiped out most traces of pre-existing culture in England – even replacing the language and religion with Latin.

The group that mainly contributed to the decline of the Roman Empire were the Scandinavians. Located primarily in Sweden, Norway, and Denmark, Scandinavia is separated from the main European continent by the Baltic Sea. Historically, the Scandinavians have been renowned seafarers. Their adventures brought them into contact with much of the rest of Europe, sometimes as feared raiders and other times as well-traveled merchants and tradesmen. One such group of Scandinavians, called the Goths, were originally from southern Sweden. They wandered south around the 1st century B.C., and settled in what is now eastern Germany and Poland. In 410 A.D., forced west by the invading Huns, the Goths sacked Rome, contributing to the decline and fall of the Western Roman Empire. As the Romans left, tribes from northern Germany and Denmark seized the opportunity to step in. The Germanic Angles and Saxons soon controlled much of the territory that had been under Roman rule, while the Jutes from Denmark occupied some smaller areas in the south. The new settlers imposed their language and customs on the local inhabitants in much the same way that the Romans had. The Germanic language spoken by the Angles would eventually develop into English.

Another group of Scandinavians who left their mark on the British Empire were the Vikings. The first waves of Vikings appeared along coastal cities and rivers, where they attacked villages, churches, monasteries, and abbeys. They would strike without warning and then quickly disappear, carrying their loot back to Scandinavia. From 793 A.D. until 1066 the Vikings explored, settled, plundered, and traded with much of Europe, Africa's Mediterranean coast, Iceland, Greenland, and the northern part of North America (Vinland). During the 9th century, Vikings established a trade port at Dublin, where they would control that area of Ireland for much of the next three hundred years. Danish Vikings invaded and settled northern and eastern England beginning in 876, and managed to control a third of Britain for nearly 80 years. In addition to laying the groundwork for new cultures and major historical events, the Vikings also left behind their DNA. In 2015, Professor Donna Heddle, Director for Nordic Studies at the University of the Highlands and Islands, stated that she believed red hair is modern evidence of the influence of ancient Vikings in Celtic lands. The prevailing idea of blonde Vikings is a myth. Statistics show that only 0.6% of the world population has red hair color. However, countries with the highest concentrations of red hair are all part of ancient Viking trading routes. In Ireland, the red hair concentrations are greatest in the areas where the Vikings settled. In looking at my relatives on the Bell tree, we seem to have a disproportionate number of redheads, based on the world-wide average. The earliest reference to red hair comes from Margaret Bell, daughter of Robert/Agnes. One history source stated Margaret has been described as having "hair like sunsets, filled with gold and red." The following Pierce brothers Ancestry.com DNA test results should shed some light on our genetics.

Regions	Edward Pierce	Robert Pierce
England, Wales, Northwestern Europe	70.00%	62.00%
Ireland, Scotland	20.00%	31.00%
Sweden, Norway	1.00%	7.00%
France	2.00%	
Germanic Europe	7.00%	

* Note: The results for Edward have been updated several times over the six years since he submitted his saliva sample. Robert's results were only recently submitted and analyzed. According to reports on DNA, siblings would have similar, but not identical percentages. Both brothers would have 50% Pierce genes and 50% Bell genes.

"Scotland" was not coined until the 9th century. According to historians at Ancestry.com, the majority of our Scots Irish ancestors emanated from the cradle of races: eastern Africa to the Euphrates, aka the Garden of Eden. Their journey continued in waves of emigration round the northern Mediterranean shores into Spain and France. The final leg of our ancestral journey went approximately 500 miles to Cornwall, Wales, and Alba, the ancient name for Scotland. The Pierce brother's DNA accurately reflects this journey. This journey took untold centuries. The greater percentage numbers reflect more recent ancestors, while the smaller numbers reflect our oldest ancestors.

Scotland is, by our American standards, a small country. In square mileage, Scotland is about the size of Maine, or South Carolina. About 60% of the country is located in what is called the Highlands. Located in the northern and western areas, plus the islands off the west coast, farming in the Highlands is difficult, at best. Poor soil and climate make this area very inhospitable. All towns, and the majority of the population, were in the Lowlands, comprising the other

40% of Scotland. In 1600, every Royal burgh in Old Scotland, was within ten miles of the sea. Today, practically every modern city is within the same ten miles.

The deplorable conditions our ancestors faced daily can hardly be imagined in our own 21st century lives. A home was likely to be little more than a shanty, constructed of stones, banked with turf, without mortar, and with straw, heather, or moss stuffed in the holes to keep out the blasts. The roof was of thatch or turf. There were no chimneys, but only holes in the roof for the smoke to escape. The fire, usually in the middle of the house floor, often filled the whole hut with foul smelling clouds, since the smoke-clotted roof gradually plugged the vent-hole. Dried manure, coal, and peat were their main sources of fuel for these fires. Just try to imagine the odor of a fire in your living room, where dried manure is your fuel for heat and cooking...Cattle were tethered at night in one end of the room, while the family lay at the other end. Floors were of the earth itself and mud and filth from the farmyard was tracked into the home. Beds were piles of heather sitting directly on the floor. Sanitary arrangements were totally lacking and since animals slept in the same room, vermin abounded. Light came in from an opening at either gable; when the wind blew and winter came, these holes were stuffed with ferns or old rags to keep out the sleet and winds. Illness was frequent and epidemics recurrent. Skin diseases were common in the dirty, dank homes. People had no idea of quarantine, so epidemics were rampant. In sick huts on the Sabbath, friends and neighbors of the sick would gather to express their sympathy, til the shanty was even more foul than normal, the sick person would be stifled by the heat, plus now the friends and neighbors were probably now infected. Smallpox and bubonic plague were rampant in these deplorable conditions. Kitchen implements were crude and few, thus food preparation was equally as squalid. For example, it was considered unlucky to wash the butter churn, so a frog was put into the tubs to make the milk churn; the consistency of butter was thought to depend on the number of hairs it contained. It was these conditions that our ancestors desired to escape, when, beginning in 1610, Ulster was opened to these Scots. Those in Scotland, who accepted the invitation, became the ancestors of all the Scots-Irish in America, including our Bells and Flemings. Those Scots, who went across the Channel to Northern Ireland to participate in the "Plantation of Ulster" from 1610 onward, went to look for a better life, to escape miserable conditions, or simply for sheer excitement.

Going back several hundred years, prior to the Nine Years War of the 1590's, Ulster was the most Gaelic part of Ireland. It was also the only province that was completely outside English control. The beginning of the Scots-Irish story began in 1603, when King James V1, the Scottish Stuart king, became James 1,

King of England, uniting those two crowns. He also gained possession of the Kingdom of Ireland, which at that time, was an English Crown possession. One of his first acts, in an attempt to rein in the unruly Catholics in Ulster, was to seize lands in Northern Ireland and grant these seized lands to Protestant Scottish landlords and English merchants. Those recipients of estates were to then persuade tenants to migrate to the northern Irish province and lease farms. In many cases, the Plantation landlords were "absentee landlords," so there was little or no personal contact with the tenants. The average lease length in Ulster was thirty one years, which was far longer than those in Scotland. This served as a major draw to those seeking lands in Ulster. However, once the thirty one year lease expired, landlords began resorting to what was known as "rack-renting." The landlord raised the land lease fees to double and even triple the initial lease. There was no loyalty to prior renters...the lease went to the person who would pay the price. The Catholic landowners in the seized northern lands of Ireland were obviously none too pleased by the King's decision, which generally made life for the new and original settlers miserable, if not down-right dangerous. The attempt to dilute the Irish population by mixing religions was adding fuel to an already simmering fire.

The earliest Bell ancestor I have definitely been able to trace our line to, is our 6th gr. Grandfather (my generation) Robert Bell. Robert and his wife, Agnes Fleming Bell, are also our original Bell immigrants to America. Robert was born in the early 1700's in County Antrim, located in the northeast section of Ulster within sight of the coast of Scotland. There are records that state the Bells lived in and around the towns of Londonderry and Derry. Today, we know them simply as Derry. Divided by a river, the town was split into two by religion, and the area has seen a turbulent and sometimes violent past. Protestants lived in Derry, while the Catholics lived in Londonderry. They even went so far as to construct a wall between the two, which did little to stem the violence. A trip to town center will give you a poignant visual reminder of Irish history.

IRISH REPUBLICAN PRISONERS WELFARE ASSOCIATION
END ISOLATION
MAGHABERRY TORTURE CAMP

KELLS WALK
THE ... ARMY
IN IRELAND
AND PALESTINE

CIVIL RIGHTS
ONE MAN ONE VOTE
JOBS NOT CREED
ANTI SECTARIAN

One of the most striking features in Derry is the Peace Bridge, which was constructed to join both sections of town, so people could walk freely back and forth over the river. What makes the bridge so compelling is the fact it is curved across the river. The reasoning behind the curve is stated on a nearby plaque "The Path to Freedom is Never a Straight Line."

In talking with Ulster residents on a recent trip, despite the violent past, there is presently only one Ireland. One of the most highly recommended tours on our trip to Belfast, was a Black Taxi Tour of the once war-torn areas. Murals on building walls, along with stories related by our driver, gave us a most interesting and vivid history of the recent past. The final stop on our tour was at the Peace Wall. Our driver handed us magic markers so we could add our names to the multitude of messages, hoping the violence is past history. *Those who do not learn history are doomed to repeat it,"* George Santayana.

Present-day Belfast Murals

While I have not been able to trace our Bell line back to Scotland, I was able to trace his wife's Fleming Clan ancestry back multiple generations. Agnes Fleming was born about 1716, in Edinburgh, Scotland, daughter of William and Martha Janet Clark Fleming, The heritage of the Fleming surname is thought to lie with the Flemish, the people of the historic county of Flanders, a territory which is presently part of France, Belgium, and the Netherlands. The Flemish emigrated to Britain in successive waves. Among the Normans who invaded England in 1066 were many Flemings, and William, the Conqueror rewarded his Flemish followers, just as he did the Normans. Many of these nobles, their ancestors and followers made their way initially to the Lanarkshire area of Scotland.

The Flemings initially in settled in Lanarkshire County around 1100 A.D., which was the most populated county in Scotland, and had larger boundaries in those days. Present-day Renfrewshire County was included in Lanarkshire, and it was in Biggar, Renfrewshire County, that the early Flemings built Boghall Castle. The Flemings fought on the side of Robert de Bruce, in his battle to free Scotland from England's rule. It is thought that Robert the Bruce gave the Flemings land in the area of Biggar in the 14th century. Considering our Agnes Fleming was born in

Edinburgh, which is only about thirty miles from Biggar, it is not inconceivable to see how our line of the original Flemings wound up in Edinburgh.

There are some Fleming surname researchers that have linked that line with royalty, including Charlemagne, and the four King James of Scotland. Being related to those notables also connects the Flemings with Henry V11, Christian 1- King of Denmark, and Robert 111 - King of Scotland, among others. It is somewhat confusing distinguishing the surname Fleming from the Flemish people. Surnames were not required until around 1100 A.D. , and some people, like our Fleming ancestors, chose their surname based on their homelands.

The Fleming Crest depicts a goat's head worn on top of the helmet. While many of us later descendants might think of a goat as an animal not worthy of a proud heritage, the head of any animal stands for honor – the head is the center of knowledge, thinking, and learning. The Fleming motto of "Let the Deed Shaw" was originally a war cry or slogan.

In addition to their fighting ability, the Flemings became the artisan industrialists of the low-countries. The economy of the British Isles could not continue to depend on agriculture and farming and survive in an industrial world, which was discovering the many economic benefits of trading. Known for their prowess in trading, the Flemings of Berwick formed a separate and influential trade-guild in that region. That influence did not go unnoticed by the English. Deciding the Flemings were gaining too much wealth, the English stormed the region in 1296. Many of the Flemings barricaded themselves in the Red Hall, and fought to their deaths. That only served as fuel in the Clans subsequent battles against the hated English. The Clan assisted Robert the Bruce in securing a victory for Scotland in 1320. The Flemings also assisted Mary, Queen of Scots with an army of 6,000 men. Unfortunately they were defeated by the English forces, leading to even more slaughtering of Flemings. Fortunately for us, some managed to survive, and have led us on an impressive genealogical journey.

From the 15th century on, came Flemish craftsmen, weavers, artisans, paper makers, glass makers, clothiers, and glove makers. During the 16th, 17th, and 18th centuries, Britain was ravaged by religious conflict. A form of Christian faith and practice developed in reaction against the established Catholic religion. Generally known as the Protestant Reformation, organized by Martin Luther, this was an attempt to reform the Catholic Church, which the followers believed to be corrupt. The resulting turmoil had a lasting impact on European politics. The religious turmoil led to warfare within most states and between many countries. Within the Protestant Movement, different religious factions began to organize. Presbyterian and Puritanism - the newly found political fervour of the followers of Oliver Cromwell, battled the more established Catholic followers - remnants of the Roman invasion, dating back to AD 43. Originally part of the Anglican Church, the recognized Church of England, the Puritans soon drew the ire of that church by their conflicting views, especially on the idea of separation of church and state. These conflicts caused many English settlers to leave England for areas where they could freely practice their religious beliefs. The Netherlands, Wales, and Scotland became "safe havens" for Puritans, Pilgrims, Quakers, and other Separatist groups seeking to escape from the Church of England. Puritans were reformers, initially trying to reform the Anglican Church from within. They had a more rational understanding of the relationship between the Church and the State. Pilgrims are also referred to as Separatists. They were once Puritans, but became upset at the lack of reforms by the Anglican Church/English Government. They decided to leave England and form their own churches. Quakers also faced persecution in England and eventually fled, seeking religious freedom. The Quakers were the most progressive, by today's standards, of the three groups that splintered off from the Protestant Movement. Quakers believed God lived inside everyone, and allowed women to participate, as well as hold leadership seats in church. Once in America, Quakers even supported the Native Americans by building numerous Native American schools, and allowed them to have leadership positions. Initially the "safe havens" in the Netherlands, Wales, and Scotland provided these religious sects their desired freedoms. However, the Anglican Church forced them to seek asylum in America. From what research I have been able to uncover, it appears that both the battle-hardened Flemings and Bells were part of this same Protestant journey.

Our Bell Clan lineage is a mystery. The earliest historical record that mentions the surname Bell dates to 1086. From what I have been able to determine, we are descended from a clan of Bells, who were labeled "Border Bells," named for their proximity to the England/Scotland border. The name Bell was common on the Scottish border for centuries, and the "Belles" are in included in the 1587 list of unruly clans in the West Marches area of the border territory. Looking back into the Bell surname history, during the period from 1066 to 1779, Bells were Normans, Nobles, Bishops, Clan Chiefs, Clergy, Merchants, Ship Captains, Simple Farmers and Herders, Inventors, Indentured Servants, and Transported Undesirables. They were active as Virginia Company of London Charter Signers, Explorers, Colony Settlers and Plantation Owners, Members of Parliament, Members of Congress, Governors, Military Officers and Soldiers, American Patriots, Slave Owners, and a Presidential Candidate. Famous people with Bell connections include Walt Disney, actress Kristen James Stewart, singers Carrie Underwood and Christina Aguilera, and our 2nd cousin 10x removed (my generation), Benjamin Franklin. And for us athletes... Derek Jeter, NY Yankees retired shortstop, and a certain Hall of Famer, is our 8th cousin 2x (my generation).

The Bells were among the earliest Scots to make the journey from their native Scotland to the promised-land in Northern Ireland. The problem I am facing in my genealogy research is that the Bell surname is the 898th most common name in Scotland. Five generations previous, each of us has thirty-two ancestors. If we go back about ten generations, which would cover roughly two hundred and fifty years, we have one thousand twenty four ancestors. Add the Scottish naming pattern to that jumble of possible relatives, and you can see what a nightmare is involved in researching Scots Irish ancestry. One historically famous possible Bell Clan ancestor is Sir Robert Bell, Speaker of the House of Commons from 1572 to 1577. Sir Bell was also Lord (Chief) Baron of the Exchequer for Queen Elizabeth I, meaning Robert was in charge the collection and administering of royal revenues. However, perhaps Robert's greatest accomplishment was fathering two separate families of twelve children each. Yikes – what a genealogical "needle in the haystack" nightmare!

The Plantations and their related agricultural development radically altered Ireland's ecology and physical appearance. In 1600, much of Ireland was heavily wooded, apart from the bogs. Most of the population lived in small townlands, many migrating seasonally to fresh pastures for their cattle. By 1700, Ireland's native woodland had been decimated; it was intensively exploited by the new settlers for commercial ventures such as shipbuilding, as much of the English forests had been destroyed and the English navy was becoming a major power. Several native species, such as the wolf, were hunted to extinction during this period. The environmental adage that "whatever you do to the environment, you ultimately do to yourselves" came back to haunt the residents of Ireland, as the settler population became urbanized. Instead of many families growing and raising their own crops and livestock, they now relied on larger farms for the potatoes and grains for the people and livestock. The Irish Famine of 1740-41 was due to extremely cold and then rainy weather for successive years. Referred to as "The Great Frost", barely any snow fell, plus rivers, lakes, and waterfalls froze, causing fish to die. Frozen quays (pronounced "keys") temporarily kept ships from ferrying coal from south Wales, so there was no fuel for warming fires. Many large cities in the island of Ireland were built on sandy fords at the mouth of rivers. Known as Quays, these waterways provided shipping transportation for both imports and exports. They were large and deep enough to allow ships to proceed to city center, thus eliminating the need to transport goods overland. Ferries also used the Quays to shuttle people to other areas in Great Britain. In Ulster, there were major Quays at Donegal and Belfast. The one pictured is the modern-day Belfast Quay.

People tried to avoid hypothermia without using up winter fuel reserves in a matter of days, by stripping bare hedges, ornamental trees, and nurseries around towns to obtain substitute fuel. The frozen rivers kept mill-wheels from operating; thus, what stored grains that did exist could not be ground into wheat for baking. When the quays opened up at the end of January, coal prices soared, putting coal out of reach of most of the residents. By the summer of 1740, the Frost had decimated the potatoes, and the drought had destroyed the grain harvest. Herds of sheep and cattle died, causing a shortage of milk and meat. Add rack-renting to the woes of the settlers, where many lost their properties and homes. Starving rural dwellers started a "mass vagrancy" towards the better-supplied towns; by mid-June, beggars lined the streets. Arrest records from that era reflect the desperate measures these people resorted to just to feed themselves and their families. The punishment for this crime was either beheading or deportation to America. Sadly, because of stories about deaths and scalpings at the hands of the Native Americans, some people actually chose to be beheaded rather than face the perils of colonial America. Fortunately for us, several Bells chose to be deported as "Undesirables."

An estimated 400,000 persons died in Ireland during 1740-41. This prompted a mass migration to America, where Ulster lost close to a quarter of its population that had been engaged in manufacturing, to the new colony. Many of the earlier immigrants came through Philadelphia, which had a large population of English settlers. The English generally viewed these Ulster-Scot immigrants as their "dirty little cousins," due to their crudeness, and love of brawling. Western Pennsylvania is a hotbed for Scots-Irish descendants. The term Scots-Irish is actually a relatively new term, coined by Americans, for Ulster Scots or Ulster-Scots people. According to the book <u>Researching Clan Bell in North America</u>, 9 major Bell families have been identified as having lived in Ulster. Of them, it is said that between the years 1707 and 1729, approximately 500 Bell families emigrated from Ulster to North America. Many Bells immigrated to the Philadelphia area, while DNA has linked Sir William Bell to Bells found in Accomack and Northampton Counties in Virginia. At any rate, Early Pennsylvania settlers, including our Bells, tended to share two things in common: they had known hardship, and they had the ambition to cross an ocean to find something better.

Lest we descendants think the crossing of the Atlantic on colonial ships was like life on our modern-day cruise ships…the depiction to the left of life on those ships ought to open your eyes. Each family was given one individual berth for the duration of the crossing, which took weeks, not days. Sanitary facilities consisted of a bucket, fresh water was minimal at best, limited or no cooking facilities, and if a person died, their body was dumped overboard. Those who survived the crossing were our hardy ancestors. Their farms turned Pennsylvania into colonial America's breadbasket, and their soldiers helped win the Revolution for the Patriots and the Civil War for the Union. By the time many of their descendants completed their assimilation into the American fabric during World War I, they had left their cultural mark from Philadelphia to Des Moines.

The Scots-Irish, realizing they could live a better life away from the British, followed a path westward and south, many to the rich Shenandoah Valley of Virginia. One trait of these hardy pioneers was that they preferred to settle where no European previously had lived. In many cases, they were the first "white settlers" in that area. This brought them in close contact with the Native Americans, with whom they occasionally clashed. As word of the fertile lands spread back to Great Britain, many more Ulster-Scots departed Ireland and sailed to America. Our Robert Bell chose to leave behind the desperate times in Ireland and sailed to America, arriving in Philadelphia around 1744. His wife, Agnes Fleming Bell, was with him, along with four young children under the age of seven. Family lore has it that two of Robert's brothers were also on the ship. No names were given, but allegedly one brother stayed in Pennsylvania and the other went south. Robert and Agnes traveled by wagon on The Great Philadelphia Wagon Road and purchased 330 acres on Patterson Creek in Romney, Virginia (now in the eastern panhandle of West Virginia). They were the first white settlers in the Romney area.

Some of the Scots-Irish engaged in farming, but many more became tavern/hotel owners, mill operators, and general store operators. The battle-hardened Scots-Irish soon made an important contribution to the fledgling colony as they enlisted in the Continental Army in the Revolutionary War. Their wilderness experiences served them well in negotiating the wilds of America, including dealing with Native American attacks, and they needed little encouragement in attacking the much-hated elite British.

Robert and Agnes Bell eventually had 10 children: eight sons and two daughters. In an era of smallpox, deadly influenza, pneumonia without antibiotics and few to no doctors and hospitals, along with many pioneer dangers, it is remarkable that all these children are believed to have survived to adulthood. To further compound the genealogy research, the children were named Margaret, John, Robert, David, Samuel, Charles, Joseph, William, James, and Jane. There is a fascinating story regarding James that I will relate later in the book. All of these are common names in the Bell lines. Hopefully DNA will eventually show us from which Bell Clan we are descended.

The French and Indian War found Robert Sr. serving in the VA Regiment under Colonel George Washington. VA Governor Dinwiddie sent Washington multiple times to scout out what was called "The Forks" (of the Ohio river). The French had established a fort there and refused to leave. At Washington's request, a force of about 400 VA recruits was assembled. One of these recruits was our ancestor, Robert Bell Sr. Marching to Pittsburgh, the French were engaged in the Battle of Great Meadows, where Robert was wounded. According to military records, Robert retired with a small one-time disability paycheck.

Perhaps it was the paycheck that enticed Robert to look for a more fertile piece of land in western Pennsylvania, and so he made several trips by horseback to scout out potential lands. He owned a fine spirited horse named Drednot, who was generally regarded as swift and sure-footed. In 1772, while returning from a scouting trip in PA, the horse's saddle girth burst, throwing Robert off. He died at the scene, while Drednot continued home without a rider. Family members immediately sent out a search party, hoping to find Robert alive. This was not the case, as it appeared Drednot's strap burst as he was jumping across a brook, causing Robert to fall head first onto rocks, killing him instantly.

The familiarity of the area around the Ohio River, plus others of the Bell surname who had settled there, lured the Bell family to sell the Romney property in 1773, and move to the Sewickley Settlement in Westmoreland County. In short time, they desired for the frontier life again, and so they relocated to Chartiers Valley near Carnegie, PA. Once again, they were the first settlers in that area.

The story about James Bell involves the perils of "living life on the edge." Mr. and Mrs. Bell had eight sons and two daughters. James Bell, Sr., the oldest, was born in 1751. When he was a small lad of ten years, his father went to Patterson Fort (1761) for a wagon load of wood. James and his brother went along, their father wanted them to gather wood while he was hauling some home. The two boys were busy gathering wood when the Indians attacked them. They caught James but his brother ran and the Indians shot at him and he fell under a log, the Indians thinking he was dead; he was not hurt, however, and later went home and told that James was captured. The Indians took James to Indiana and kept him there till he was returned by treaty. When his father went after him he took two horses that James might ride home. When they met, James got on the horse but had ridden only a short distance when he saw a woman and some children who were also set free. James dismounted, letting the woman ride. "When he arrived home it was at night. His mother, hearing the wooden latch lift with a string, called: 'Is that you, James?' and his father answered, "Yes." It was a joyful meeting. James had many stories to relate of his capture. Among them was one that revealed when Indians took him to the Ohio River, they made a canoe and put him in it, and they had nothing to eat except what they called 'cush meat.' He always claimed they crossed into Pennsylvania and came through Chartiers Valley, near Chartiers Creek. He told how they would have two lines of Indians and would make him run between the lines, which we now know as a "gauntlet." An old Indian squaw became angry if they struck him, but he was a fast runner and did not get struck often. They pulled all his hair out of the top of his head and put rings in his ears. After he had been with them awhile the Indians became very friendly with him, and when he left, the old Indian squaw cried. Once reunited with his Bell family, James lived with his mother, but the traits of the Indians never left him. He would gladly exchange his white man's clothes for the Indian costume and take himself to the woods to hunt and fish.

Several generations of Bells were raised in the Pittsburgh area. Edna's 2 gr grandfather, John Bell, was born in Virginia on the 28th of January 1770, and when but an infant, was taken by his family to Pittsburgh where he resided until 1800. At the age of 30, John struck out on his own, following the age-old tradition of preferring pioneer living. John moved his family to the vicinity of what is now the town of Indiana, where he was, in 1805 on the formation of Indiana County, elected the first constable in the county. In 1809 he decided to penetrate still further into the wilderness and claimed land about one mile north of the Big

Mahoning Creek, where he built the first dwelling in that part of present-day
Jefferson county. Until the year 1812, his nearest neighbors to the south were nine
miles into Indiana county, and the nearest to the north, in what is now Jefferson
county, were those living in the Barnett Settlement, a distance of over twenty
miles.

For a long time after Mr. Bell took up his abode in this wilderness, his rifle,
in the use of which he was adept, was the only source of subsistence for himself
and family. The first years were spent hunting and clearing his heavily timbered
land. As a proof of his skill as a hunter it is stated, by written account, that during
his residence in Jefferson county John Bell killed two panthers, ninety-three
wolves, three hundred and six bears, and over six hundred deer, to say nothing of
wild turkeys, which were then very numerous, and other small game. The red men,
too, yet lurked in the forests, and though we usually hear nothing but friendly
actions towards the early settlers, it is stated that on one occasion Mr. Bell, who
had been to Port Barnett on business, and was obliged to camp out for the night on
his way home, saw an Indian taking aim at him from behind a tree. In relating this
incident he remarked,"that Indian was never seen afterwards" from which it was
easily inferred that the savage fell before his unerring rifle.

In 1818 Governor Findley appointed Bell Justice of the Peace, an office which
he held for twenty-five years, and in which his jurisdiction was honest and
credible. He was known throughout this region as "Squire Bell." One of Mr. Bell's
strongest characteristics was his love of truth and his sterling honesty. He would
call no man friend whom he could not respect, and he didn't try to conceal his
opinions or dislikes. For those whom he called a friend, he would make any
sacrifice of personal convenience. He was the true epitome of the early American
pioneer.

But - while he was famous as a hunter and woodsman, he did not neglect his
farm, upon which "he worked so zealously that he soon had it under a good state of
culture. Long before he was obliged to relinquish the control of it, he had made it
productive, erected comfortable buildings, and planted one of the finest orchards in
the county." When the evening came, he was able to "sit under his own vine and
fig tree; to look out over the fertile fields, which he had reclaimed from the dense
wilderness, and enjoy the fruit from the trees of his own planting."
Marriage gave our Bell line even stronger Scots-Irish ties. Squire Bell married
Elizabeth Welsh, whose lineage goes back to early Virginia. Squire John's son,
Joseph, married Sarah McKee, whose lineage contains Shawnee, as well as Scots-
Irish. It was the Shawnee connection that prompted the DNA testing on our Bell

line. Conflicting reports on the Shawnee ancestor stated that 1) yes, she was actually Shawnee, or B) she was a white captive. Since neither Bell descendant has Native American genes, it is safe to assume she was a white captive. Yet, I wonder if any relatives on that side were bullied by name-calling, such as "Pocahontas." More recently, James Todd married Elizabeth Mahaffey. It is this Mahaffey line that takes us back to Roger Williams, the founder of Rhode Island in 1636. James Todd's granddaughter, Elizabeth Drum Todd, is the wife of John Taylor Bell and the mother of Edna Todd Bell. There are pages later in this book dedicated to these Indiana County ancestors.

It appears there was a family tradition of naming children after famous persons of that era, or famous ancestors. President Zachary Taylor, our 12th President (1849-1850) is a distant Bell relative, as is Benjamin Franklin. John Squire Bell's brother, Joseph Bell, named a son Franklin Bell, and so on the surface it does appear John Taylor Bell may have been named after President Taylor, who died several years before Edna's father was born. However, with the Scottish naming pattern, plus the large families the earlier Bells produced, we can speculate that the middle name was frequently the only way to distinguish individuals with the same given names. It seems the Taylor middle name mystery may be closer to home than we think. See the page on John Taylor Bell for my hypotheses on the source of the elusive Taylor middle name.

Backtracking to Robert and Agnes Bell, the terrains of both Scotland and, especially Ireland are very suited to sheep farming. Thin, rocky soils on steep slopes with ample grasses, plus close proximity to climate modifying and moisture-producing oceans make for ideal stock raising conditions. For centuries families relied on gardening near their homesteads for vegetables, and grazing sheep on the hillsides for meat and wool for clothing. Once World markets opened up, the Irish realized they could make a prosperous living by selling lamb and mutton to other countries, plus Irish wool became a desired product for weaving and clothing, and as such, commanded a hefty price on the World market. The Irish in Ulster became some of the wealthiest people in all of Great Britain, which did not go unnoticed by the English merchants. These merchants complained to the English government that they were unable to compete fairly with the wealthy Irish. True to past and future history, the Government of Great Britain took measures to control and dilute the wealth and power of the Irish merchants. Their solution was to pass legislation stating that the Irish merchants could no longer sell on the World market. Instead, the merchants could only sell their wool and meat to the English Government...and at a reduced price! Does this sound like the more familiar future Boston Tea Party? The regulations on meat and wool weren't about taxes (tariffs?), but about control. Is it any wonder the Scots and Irish hated the English?

       Was our Robert Bell affected by the regulations on sheep? The answer may be found in the history of his wife, Agnes Fleming. Agnes was born and raised in Edinburgh, Scotland. The surname Fleming was first documented in Flanders, now present day Belgium/Luxembourg. The meaning of the name translates to "shepherd"... One can easily speculate that the Bells raised their own sheep and had the skills to operate a loom to weave flax and wool. In the early records of Virginia, Robert Bell was listed as a farmer. According to tax records, the Bells raised cattle, adding speculation to the raising of sheep. They would have used the cattle to earn a living, but it would make sense guessing the family kept sheep for their own use. This pioneer family had ten children, all of whom survived to adulthood. Keeping a large family in food and clothing in the frontier would have been a full-time job, and beyond the financial means of a pioneer family. There were no Walmarts or Dollar Generals back in those days!

The Stark Natural Beauty of Ulster...The Giant's Causeway

The Causeway was formed around 50-60 million years ago when the area was subjected to intense volcanic activity. The molten basalt was forced through chalk beds to form a lava plateau. When it cooled about 40,000 interlocking basalt columns were left. As the basalt weathered, the tops of the columns form stepping stones that lead from the cliff foot and disappear under the sea. In 2005 the site was named as the fourth greatest natural wonder in the United Kingdom.

Located in County Antrim, on the northern coast of Ulster on the North Atlantic - the inlet that leads to Derry is located here. At the closest points between Scotland and Ulster, the distance is only 12 miles. Our ancestors would have sailed past these basalt columns. Perhaps these columns would have been looked at as a symbol of pride - representing the strength and fortitude they would need to deal with unknown obstacles. One visit to an Irish pub, where musicians are playing folk music, will leave you with a deeper understanding of the pride the Irish have in their freedom, and the cost of that freedom.

Slieve League Sea Cliffs

The highest point of these cliffs reaches 1,972' – making them the highest in Europe. Our tour guide said the locals refer to these cliffs as being "twice the height" (as the Cliffs of Moher – their more famous cousin on the west coast of southern Ireland) – "and half the hype!"

If the cliffs along the island country of Ireland could talk, they would have a wealth of stories to relate. Shipwrecks from the Spanish Armada have been found off the northern coast, as well as Viking ships. Many coastal people with Irish roots, including our Bell line, also have Scandinavian and Iberian Peninsula roots. Other early invasions came from the Normans, located in present-day France and Belgium. So our DNA results stating "Europe West" could be from this source.

Picturesque View of Irish Terrain

Once wooded, this view gives you a better idea of the rough terrain, carved out by ancient glaciers, into which our ancestors laid out their plantations. The lighter green color in the bottom of the valley indicates a source of water for livestock, crops, and people alike. Remnants of the once-forested steep hillsides, now plentiful lush grasslands, are suitable for sure-footed ruminants. Who needs wooden fences when there is an abundance of stone?

Present-Day Pasture With Wooden Fence

The Bridge of Tears

Approximately 6 miles from Dunfanaghy, there is an attractive little stone bridge, which most people pass over nowadays, without a second thought. But if you look more carefully, and pay attention to the nearby plaque, your curiosity may be raised somewhat. The plaque is written in Irish, and a rough translation into English would be, "Friends and relatives of the person emigrating would come this far. Here they said their goodbyes.... This is the Bridge of Tears".

Long before the building of the railway or modern roads, this was the most common route leading from this area to Derry, and hence to the ships which would take them to England, Scotland, Australia and America. The relatives of those emigrating would accompany them along the long walk up towards Muckish Gap, and here their goodbyes would be said. There were no "See you soon"s or "Catch you later"s.The departure was treated like a death, for they would never be seen again. Crossing The Bridge had a finality for those who left, and for those who were left behind. Many tears were shed in this lonesome place. A simple plaque in stone beside the bridge reads:

"Fad leis seo a thagadh cairde agus lucht gaoil an té a bhí ag imeacht chun na coigrithe. B'anseo an scaradh. Seo Droichead na nDeor."

("Family and friends of the person leaving for foreign lands would come to this point. Here was the separation. This is the Bridge of Tears".)

These early Scots Irish have been described as a "decapitated society" by historians. Those immigrants were usually either those dissatisfied at home, or eager to improve their lives. These were immigrants - virtually no royalty, no aristocracy, no leisure class. Practically no bishops, or judges, or scientists, or even great statesmen made the journey to America. With insignificant exceptions, the highest ranking educated people, those with the highest professions, and those highly skilled craftsmen, all stayed at home. They were already successful, and as such, had no reason to go to the wilderness to start afresh. This is doubly true with our Scots Irish ancestors, as they immigrated twice. The move from Scotland to Ireland was made by the optimistic poor; the move to America once more left behind most of those who had risen to prominence.

Jefferson/Indiana, PA County Bells

Hugh McKee Bell – father of John T. Bell

Eleanor Martin Bell – mother of John T. Bell

John Taylor Bell was born 16 September 1853 in Frostburg, PA. Located in Jefferson County near Punxsutawney, on what was known as the Bell Homestead, farming was the Bell livelihood. One of seven children born to Hugh McKee Bell and Eleanor Martin Bell, J.T. Bell received his early education in the schools of the township, and in the various summer schools, which were conducted through the country for those preparing to teach, as there were no "normal schools" at that time. A quote from Stewart's 1913 Indiana County Pennsylvania states:

"John Taylor Bell belongs to a family whose history in this part of Pennsylvania begins in pioneer days, and whose members have been typical representatives of the hardy, thrifty Scotch-Irish race to which they belong. The State has this element to thank for many of its most desirable citizens. Combining intellectual vigor and strong moral qualities with physical sturdiness, they faced the hardships of the early days courageously, made the most of their opportunities,

inaugurated movements for the advancement of the general good as soon as prosperity relieved them from the pressure of unremitting devotion to their immediate needs, and helped to establish a civilization which reflects credit on all who have taken part in its accomplishment."

Two of John's brothers were dentists, while one sister was married to a physician, so it was obvious the value the parents placed on education. He started teaching at age 16, at what was later known as the Pickering Run School, in East Mahoning township, Indiana County. He remained there one year, and taught in several different schools in Indiana County for ten years, including the summer program for teachers in Plumville. When he came to Indiana, he was assistant to the principal and taught for three years. He would meet and marry (in 1885) his fellow teacher/wife, Lizzie Drum Todd during that stint in Indiana. During his teaching career, J.T. also attended the normal school in Indiana and Union College in Alliance, Ohio, after which he read law with Hon. Silas M. Clark and John N. Banks, both of Indiana. In 1886, J.T. was admitted to the bar in Indiana County, and for two years practiced law. According to his daughter, outdoor life appealed more to him than an office life, so he gave up the legal practice and turned back to the education field. This time, it was not back to the classroom...he became a salesman of school books, representing first, the firm of Porter and Coates, of Philadelphia, later with the Werner Company of Akron, OH. and lastly the American Book Company. He remained active in the Indiana community, as one of the Directors of the Indiana Savings & Trust Company, the Indiana Lodge, and was President of the Men's Social Club of Indiana. There was no explanation as to the last activity, so we will leave it at that. Reverting back to the education field, of which he obviously placed great value, J.T. was a member of the Indiana school board for over twenty five years, including being elected president several times.

John Taylor Bell passed away on 18 October 1926, at the age of 73. He was living with our Grandparents, William E. and Edna B. Pierce, at the time of his passing. The house was located at 514 School Street and had a wrap-around porch, which was later removed. Note: School Street is presently a one way street – the opposite direction from the car in the picture.

Solving the mystery of the Taylor middle name

As stated before, it appears there was a family tradition of naming children after famous persons of that era, or famous ancestors. President Zachary Taylor, our 12th President (1849-1850) is a distant Bell relative, as is Benjamin Franklin. John Squire Bell's brother, Joseph Bell, named a son Franklin Bell, so does this mean Squire John Bell named his son, John Taylor Bell, after President Taylor? #12 had died several years before J.T. was born...so this is a possibility. Examining early Indiana County history, I am throwing out an alternative logical answer. Given the historical Scottish naming pattern, plus the large families the earlier Bells produced, we can speculate that the middle name was frequently the only way to distinguish individuals with the same given names. It seems the Taylor middle name mystery may be closer to home than a military hero President.

A look at the Taylor family history follows a similar path as our Bell history...the Taylor line in the Indiana area also had their origins in Scotland. John Taylor came to the Philadelphia area in the 1740's. Alexander Taylor, son of John, was born in 1756. A surveyor by profession, Alexander settled first in Bedford County, then moved west to what is now Indiana County before 1790. He purchased a farm four miles south of the present-day borough of Indiana. Greenwood Cemetery, located on 119 south of Indiana, was originally part of the Taylor family farm. Future Taylors, of which there were many, produced many citizens of notable worth. Some Taylors followed the family profession of surveying, but later branched out as members of the Pennsylvania Legislature and Forty-third Congress; Associate Judges; Sheriffs, Lawyers, Doctors, even the editor of the first paper in Indiana. One descendant of the original John Taylor, his grandson, which, thanks to the Scottish naming pattern, was also John Taylor.

It is my belief that this John is the initial source of the Taylor middle name in our Bell line. John Taylor was one of the leading men of Indiana County in his day, holding many of the highest offices: prothonotary, county treasurer, member of the Legislature, and associate judge. He was also deputy surveyor, and surveyor general of Pennsylvania. John's son, Alexander Wilson Taylor, veered away from the surveying profession, and became a lawyer instead. His choices of schools are interesting and relevant: Jefferson College (later Washington Jefferson) for undergraduate, and Dickinson Law School for postgraduate. Both colleges were selected by future lawyers in the Bell/Pierce line.
Indiana County was formed in 1803 out of lands from Westmoreland County to the south, and Lycoming County to the north. In 1806, an act was passed to

organize the legal matters of this new county. Squire John Bell was elected the first constable of Indiana county, a position he held from 1806 to 1809. This would have put the Bells and Taylors, and their descendants, in the same area at the same time. A coincidence perhaps, but the evidence is compelling. Squire Bell's son Hugh McKee Bell, father of John Taylor Bell, was born in 1826, and would have grown up at the height of the Taylor political period. It was at this point that the Taylor-Bell connection seems to have come together.

Sarah Jane Bell, of Westmoreland County - daughter of John and Rebecca Hanson Bell, would provide the Bell/Taylor link. She was born @1824...our Hugh M. Bell was born in 1826. Tracing Sarah Bell's line, I was able to determine that her original immigrant from Ireland was Walter Bell. Walter was born @1712 in Ireland and sailed to Philadelphia, where he was warranted a tract of land, consisting of approximately 240 acres in Hanover Township in Lancaster County. There is a record of three Bell families living in that area before 1740. The heads of these families were Thomas b. @ 1710, Walter b. @ 1712, and William b. @ 1706. There is reason to believe that Thomas and Walter were brothers. As we know that our Robert Bell, b between 1700-1710, came to Philadelphia with several brothers, it is easy to speculate that these were the brothers, and would also explain how the Philadelphia Bells wound up later in Westmoreland County with our Robert Bell descendants. Sarah Jane Bell married Robert Cromwell Taylor. Taylor was one of more prominent businessmen in the Indiana borough. After retiring from the mercantile business, Taylor was named Postmaster of Indiana. His final occupation also linked him with our Pierce line. When Farmer's Bank was organized in 1876, Robert Taylor was hired as a cashier. The connection of the Taylors to Farmer's Bank has been well-documented, and, according to family lore, Attorney William E. Pierce, husband of Edna Todd Bell, was instrumental in keeping the Farmer's Bank afloat during the Great Depression in the 1930's. Sarah and Robert Taylor had three children that survived to adulthood. True to the traditional Scottish naming pattern, a couple's second son was named for the mother's father. Hence, their son, born in 1851, was named John Bell Taylor.

I have found no evidence that Hugh McKee and Eleanor Martin followed traditional naming patterns exactly in the middle names of their seven children. According to a book on Scottish history, the traditional naming pattern should be used as a rough guide, since *"no two families are exactly the same. In many cases there will be no rhyme or reason behind the names chosen for your ancestors as there were plenty of families who didn't care one bit about such traditions and their child could have been named after a dear friend, a celebrated public figure or even a popular local minister."* This appears to be the case in our line with John

Taylor Bell, who was born in 1853. The given name John was in honor of Hugh's father, Squire John Bell.

As an adult, John Bell Taylor worked at Farmer's, working his way up from cashier to Vice President. He was also Treasurer of Indiana borough, plus he was Treasurer of the Indiana School Board for a number of years. Our John Taylor Bell was born in 1853, so their ages were only about 1½ years apart. John T. Bell was also a member of the Indiana School Board for over twenty five years, and was President at the time John B.Taylor was Treasurer. Cousin Anne – school board membership must run in our genes?

Elizabeth "Lizzie" Drum Todd

Elizabeth Drum Todd, wife of John Taylor Bell, was born 5 June 1854, the first child born to William A. Todd and Susan Drum Todd. Her brother, James Todd, was two years younger. She is our connection to yet another Scots Irish military line. Like the Bells and Flemings, the Todds were renowned Scottish Border freedom fighters, and followed the same path through Ulster to America. Lizzie's father, Wm. A. Todd, read law with Judge Thomas White and was admitted to the Bar. He was associated with Edward Hutchison in Cambria County, in a law firm. At the age of 22, he enlisted in December of 1846, to fight in the Mexican War. Wm. was commissioned a 1st Sgt, and according to records at the National Archives, he was reduced to the rank of Private in January 1847. By December of 1847, he was appointed 2nd Lt, and resigned in June 1848. I point out those dates and ranks because they do not match up with future documents, including those in his obituary. He refers to himself as Colonel Wm A. Todd, and claimed to be the first person over the wall at Chapultepec. I could find nothing in his military records to substantiate his claims. At any rate, he went back to the law firm after the War and relocated to Indiana, married Susan Drum, and started a family.

Lizzie knew tragedy early in life. Her father died from liver failure in 1860 at the age of 36, before Lizzie turned six. Her ancestry, according to family legend, includes Mary Todd Lincoln. I have not been able to substantiate that legend, but I did uncover the link to Roger Williams, founder of Rhode Island. Lizzie became a teacher, one of the few professions available to women in those days. She was a teacher for many years in the Indiana public schools, where she met her future husband, the aforementioned John Taylor Bell. John Bell was also a teacher, and served as assistant principal. Perhaps she met him while escorting some unruly young man to the office, during the time of a full moon! At any rate, they were married on September 15, 1885, when Lizzie was at the advanced age of 31. As with her daughter ten years later, once a woman married, she was forced to resign from teaching.

Tragedy struck again several times during her teaching career. In 1872 her paternal grandfather passed away. In 1878 her brother James committed suicide while a cadet at West Point. And her maternal grandfather Henry Drum died in 1879. Henry and Susan Drum lived in a house on the corner of 7th and Philadelphia Streets, which many of us remember as the site of Brody's

Department Store. At some point, according to stories told by both my mother and grandmother, Lizzie Todd fell through the floor in this home, injuring herself. They both blamed the later onset of breast cancer on that accident. We now know that injury isn't a cause of breast cancer, but it is easy to understand why they felt that way in those days. See the included *Clark House News* article for more on the history of the building.

Once a woman married, she was expected to assume a role of domesticity and selflessness. The cliché of the day was that "women were to live for others." Apparently Lizzie was comfortable in this role, as she became an active worker in the Methodist Church. In this role, she must have been drawn into one of the most devastating "natural" disasters America has ever known. On May 31, 1889, between 5-10 inches of rain fell on western Pennsylvania, causing an earthen dam on South Forks to collapse. The resulting flood wiped out the neighboring community of Johnstown, causing bodies to be found as far away as Cincinnati, Ohio. Certainly she would have been highly active in the humanitarian work and relief efforts that were extended to Indiana's neighbor in the salvage and subsequent rebuilding efforts. It certainly isn't out of the question that she would have either known one or more out of the 2,000 people that perished, or have known a relative of those people.

Her daughter, Edna Todd Bell, was born on October 4, 1890, and her son, Hugh Todd Bell was born two years later. During the eleven to thirteen years with her children, they experienced Nellie Bly becoming the first woman to travel around the world alone in 72 days; baseball became a popular sport; jello and cotton candy were created, along with Tootsie Rolls. Annie Oakley and Barnum and Bailey Circus acts became popular, and one would have to wonder what they thought of Maria Spelterini crossing of Niagara Falls on a tightrope – wearing 38 pound weights on each ankle!

The year of her death saw many new inventions and happenings. The telephone, phonograph, and ice cream cones were invented, while work had begun on the Panama Canal and NY City Subways. Lizzie would not live to experience any of these modern inventions and wonders though. With the diagnosis of breast cancer, Lizzie traveled to Philadelphia in February, where she underwent one of the first mastectomies in the US (according to my mother). One can only imagine what those early surgical techniques must have been like, especially without antibiotics and only crude anesthetics. In late April, she traveled to a hospital in New York City, in an effort to conquer, or at least slow down the ravaging effects of the disease. The cancer must have been advanced because she lived less than 6 months after the initial mastectomy, passing away on June 4, 1904 – one day short of her 50th birthday.

The surname Todd could be a nickname for someone resembling a fox, either by his slyness or cunning, or by his red hair, or he could be a fox hunter. Todd is both an English and a Scottish surname. DNA testing suggests that the English Todds tended to be of European descent, while the Scottish Todds were Nordic. Since our Todd line is Scottish, the Nordic lineage fits into the red hair theory of Professor Donna Heddle, mentioned earlier in this book. The earliest Todd I can definitively link our line to is James Todd and his wife Mary Spence Todd. James was born in Belfast, Ulster, Ireland in 1769, married Mary Spence, also of Belfast around 1787. Their son James Todd, was born in Belfast on 22 February 1788. The family immigrated to America in 1789, where they made their home in Chambersburg, Franklin County, PA. The elder James died shortly after that, and is buried there. Mary remarried Patrick Sheridan, and they, along with James Jr. relocated, by an oxen driven wagon to a farm in Westmoreland County.

James married Elizabeth Mahaffey in 1808, and they farmed in Westmoreland County until 1815. The Todds then moved to Indiana County, where they purchased a farm and farmed until Elizabeth passed away in 1842, at the relatively young age of 55. James remarried in 1844 and then relocated to the town of Indiana, where he opened a mercantile. James was active politically in Indiana County, as well as the community of Indiana. He served as County

Commissioner 1826-1828, County Treasurer 1833-1835. In 1837, he was elected a member of the Pennsylvania Constitutional Convention. He was politically an Anti Mason from 1831 on, and later was a Whig in 1852. He helped secure the extension of the Pennsylvania Railroad to Indiana, served as trustee of the Indiana Seminary 1858-59, elected as one of the first directors at the organization of the Indiana Co. Mutual Fire Insurance Co. in 1862, member of the Indiana Council 1848-1850, and Burgess (Mayor) of Indiana 1853-54. He was an early temperance advocate from about 1815-23. A busy man, James was also active in his church, the Indiana Presbyterian Church, as an Elder for many years.

It is our 2nd great grandmother (my generation) Elizabeth Mahaffey's line that links us with Roger Williams, founder of Rhode Island. In tracing the Mahaffey line back, I found the same path the Bell/Fleming line took through Ulster. The Mahaffey's were from Donegal, came through Philadelphia, and eventually settled in Westmoreland County. Going back further on the line, I came upon the Cranston surname, including Samuel and John Cranston, both Governors of Rhode Island. Also on that line is our 9th Gr. Grandmother, Freeborn Williams, born 1635 in Salem, MA, daughter of Roger Williams and Mary Barnard Williams. Roger then is our 10th gr. grandfather, and notable for being a staunch advocate for religious freedom, separation of church and state, and fair dealings with American Indians, and he was one of the first abolitionists. Born in London, 21 December 1603, he must have been aware of the numerous burnings at the stake that had taken place at nearby Smithfield of so-called Puritans or heretics. This probably influenced his later strong beliefs in civic and religious liberty. He came to the attention of Sir Edmund Coke, a brilliant lawyer and one-time Chief Justice of England. Through Coke's influence, Roger was entered first in a Charter House school, and later Pembroke College at Cambridge University. While at Pembroke, Williams was one of eight granted scholarship recipients, based on excellence in Latin, Greek, and Hebrew. Graduating in 1627, Roger became Chaplain to a wealthy family. Even at a young age, Williams began to draw attention and the ire of Puritans because of his views on freedom of worship. Learning about the Plymouth Colony in Massachusetts, Roger and his wife deemed it prudent to leave England and sail to America. They sailed in 1630, ten years after the Pilgrims landed at Plymouth, arriving 5 February 1631 at Boston in the Massachusetts Bay Colony. As soon as Roger arrived in Boston, he was offered the post of teacher in a Boston church. New England Puritan churches divided the minister's role between two people, one called the pastor and one the teacher. To their surprise Roger turned down the job because the Boston church was not "separated" formally from the Anglican church, and therefore was not pure enough for his beliefs. He preached first at Salem, then at Plymouth, then back to Salem, always at odds with the structured Puritans. When he got word that he would be banished from the colony, and shipped back to England, in January, Williams fled southwest out of the Massachusetts Bay Colony and was befriended by local Indians. The Narragansett Indians helped Williams survive the winter. Williams purchased land from the Narragansett chiefs, and named his settlement Providence, in thanks to God. He believed that all human beings were equal in the eyes of God and carried out this belief throughout his life in his dealings with the Natives.

Roger made several trips back to England to obtain a Charter for his growing Providence colony. He was elected Governor of the Colony 1654 through 1658, continued to preach, and the Colony grew through its acceptance of settlers of all religious persuasions. Roger died at Providence sometime between January and March, 1683. His descendants have contributed in many ways: first to the establishment of an independent Colony, and later to the establishment of an independent state, Rhode Island, in a united nation. Though under attack recently, the United States of America has maintained the reality of separation of church and state which Roger Williams envisioned, and ordained in his settlement at Providence. So while Roger Williams was not Scots Irish, his path to America was based on finding religious freedom, similar to our Scots Irish ancestors, and thus his story is definitely one of courage and determination.

This is the April 2018 issue of *Clark House News*, which features the history of the building on the northeast corner of Philadelphia and 7th Street in Indiana, PA. that housed Brody's Department Store. This is the same building where Lizzie Todd Bell fell through the second floor and injured herself.

Clark House News

Monthly Publication of the Historical & Genealogical Society of Indiana County

www.hgsic.org   April 2018   ichistoricalsociety@gmail.com

The History of Brody's Corner
by Clarence D. Stephenson

The story of what has been known for years as "Brody's Corner" at Seventh and Philadelphia Streets in Indiana begins with William Lucas, a tailor prior to 1810. He appears to have erected the first house at an early date. Lucas served two terms as treasurer of the county, was on the Borough Council several years and was burgess in 1827. In 1821 and some years afterward he was treasurer of the Indiana and Ebensburg Turnpike Road Co., which operated an old-style toll road along Route 422 from Indiana to Ebensburg. By 1833 he was a justice of the peace. After that date nothing more is known so it may be presumed he either moved or was deceased.

By the time of David Peelor's map of Indiana in 1855, William A. Todd is listed as residing on Lot No. 5, corner of Vine and Philadelphia Streets. Vine Street was later named Seventh Street. A veteran of the Mexican War, Todd was an attorney and it is likely that his office was at this location. The 1871 Beer's Atlas of Indiana County indicates Henry Drum on the "Brody Corner." Drum was then deceased, so the actual resident was most likely his daughter, Susan, who had married William Todd in 1861. Susan was survived by a daughter, Elizabeth Todd, who married John Taylor Bell, a prominent businessman and a director of the Indiana Savings & Trust Company.

From about 1893, Jacob B. Younkins had been renting the street floor as a grocery. A barber shop also occupied part of the space. Then in November 1908 it was announced Younkins was selling the contents of the store and had workmen razing the rear part of the building preparatory to opening a nickelodeon known as the "Star Theater." Nickelodeons showed silent movies, usually accompanied by a piano. Admission was 5 cents, hence "nickelodeon." A 10 x 15-foot stage was built at the rear of the building adjoining a Chinese laundry. Three dressing rooms opened onto the stage. There were four sets of scenery and a drop curtain with business advertisements surrounding a pretty lake scene—all painted by A. S. Work of Punxsutawney.

The hall had three exits, one on Seventh Street, and a raised floor sloping toward the stage. Paneled walls, rows of electric lights and opera chairs were additional interior features. The seating capacity was 150. At the front was a box office and over it a large star with thirty incandescent lights. The overall dimensions of the theater were 20 by 60 feet.

The Star Theater opened December 21, 1908. The Pfeil Twins, singing and dancing comediennes, were booked by the Gus Sun Agency of Pittsburgh. The feature movie was "The Auto Heroine." In addition to Mr. Younkins, as manager, the staff consisted of William Klingensmith, electrician; Miss Rose Trainor, pianist; Andrew Hasinger, violinist; and W. Parke Younkins, ticket seller. In November 1909 the Star featured thirty minutes of the World Series baseball game between the Pittsburgh Pirates and Detroit Tigers. Younkins continued the Star Theater over six years. On April 17, 1915, he announced the theater would close for "an indefinite period."

Society Calendar

April 3 - Board of Directors meeting, 5:00 pm, Helman Library

April 7 - Spring work day on the grounds

April 28 - Ladies' Tea at the Clark House

Hyman J. and Israel I. Brody had rented the building from J. T. Bell and opened a clothing store later that year. Previously, Israel had initiated Brody's on March 15, 1913 in the Thomas Flat Building on the east side of the Moore Hotel. Hyman had been in the clothing business in Punxsutawney since 1911, but closed that store to go into partnership with Israel. The business grew and expanded. The Bell Building was purchased and enlarged in 1920 to an adjoining brick building. In June 1934 they purchased the Harry White Building. The Hub Store had occupied the ground floor of the White Building since 1912 until sometime prior to the Brody purchase.

North Seventh St., Indiana, looking toward Vinegar Hill. The Star Theater on right opened Dec. 21, 1908.

In August 1937 it was announced that Brody's would buy the Second United Presbyterian Church building on Seventh Street at the rear of the Brody store and planned to lower it to street level and connect it to the store. This was finally completed in 1943. In 1896 the Second U. P. congregation purchased this lot from J. T. Bell for $1,250. The congregation had split off from the First U. P. Church (now Graystone) in 1894 because of a controversy over the installation of a pipe-tuned reed organ.

The Clark House News
Volume XXIV Number 4 - 2018
A monthly publication of the
Historical & Genealogical Society
of Indiana County
621 Wayne Avenue
Indiana, Pennsylvania 15701-3072
Telephone: 724-463-9600
www.hgsic.org
E-mail: ichistoricalsociety@gmail.com
Library Hours:
Tuesday-Friday, 9:00-4:00
Saturday: 10:00-3:00
2018 Board of Directors
President: JoAnne McQuilkin
Vice President: Mary Yanity
Treasurer: Herb Gleditsch
Secretary: Clerissa Connelly

Samantha Barna	Shirley Dill
Vincent Beatty	Katie Gaudreau
Don Becker	Joe Hildebrand
Gary Clawson	Bruce Jenkins
Tom Crumm	Dorie Leathers
Eugene Decker	Jackie Wiley
Joe Dell	

Jonathan Bogert, Executive Director
Jean Williams, Director Emeritus
Dorie Leathers, Editor

Expansion continued in 1952 with excavations under the Harry White Building which added more basement space. A major place took change the following year with the acquisition of partnership interests by the sons of Hyman and Israel. Brody Brothers became the only Indiana-owned and Indiana-operated department store. There were departments for shoes, men's wear, ladies' wear, children and youth, piece goods and home furnishings.

At some point in the 1970s, Brody Brothers acquired the old *Indiana Progress* building which stood at the corner of Seventh Street and Nixon Avenue behind the Brody store. The *Progress,* founded in 1870, was a well-known weekly newspaper in Indiana. A new three-story building was erected in 1896, and here the paper was published until its last issue on April 14, 1946. The building was demolished sometime later and in 1975 Brody Brothers constructed a 48 x 90-foot addition on the site from Seventh Street along Nixon Avenue as far as G.C. Murphy Company (now the Atrium).

The original Brody's store

The Brody story began with Abraham Brody, the founder of the family in America, who was born n 1864 in Lithuania where he married Sarah David. They emigrated in 1886, arriving in New York City. He took up peddling of wares door to door and lived for a time in Blossburg, Tioga County. In 1898 he opened a general store in Ralston, Lycoming County. Then, attracted by the coal boom, he moved to Anita in Jefferson County in 1900 and opened a store there. He helped his sons, Hyman and Israel, get started in business.

In 1915 Abraham Brody opened a general store in Rossiter and continued there until 1940 when he retired. He resided in Punxsutawney until his death in 1945 at age 81. His life epitomized the success of many immigrants who fled from the oppression of poverty of the Old World to the freedom and hope of the New World. His descendants have been a credit to him and to the communities where they lived, and to Indiana in particular. Hyman and Israel were founding members of the Indiana County Chamber of Commerce and the Indiana Merchants Association and their descendants served as founding members of the Indiana County Guidance Center, presidents of the William Penn Council, Boy Scouts, chairmen of the Indiana County March of Dimes, directors of the Indiana County Red Cross, and served in the U. S. Navy and Air Force.

When Brody Brothers closed its doors in November of 1987, the family ended 74 years in the business life of Indiana.

From the Executive Director
Jonathan Bogert
ichistoricalsociety@gmail.com

As April showers roll in, there are multiple events taking place at the Society and plenty of projects underway. Our intern presses on through the second half of the semester while she grows familiar with our collections and volunteers. Organization continues to take place at the museum inside and out as the Society takes advantage of any favorable weather that comes its way. The HGSIC is also cleaning things up from an administrative standpoint as new policy and procedure make their way into practice. These projects help the Society prepare for its busiest time of the year, which is rapidly approaching.

Last month at the Armory, board members **Joe Hildebrand** and **Joe Dell** presented a program for the Trail Life scout group which touched on elements of Civil War history. Participants learned about life in camp, combat, and the proper procedure to follow when firing a cannon. The Society was thrilled at the level of interest the group had and was pleased with the many questions posed after the presentation. This event served as preparation for next month when the Society collaborates with Horace Mann Elementary during their annual Civil War encampment. As the Society expands its educational offerings, we are always looking for educators interested in contributing to the program.

Trail Life scouts enjoy Civil War history program

A scheduled work day starts off projects for the month of April, as the Society looks to mulch, trim, and remove debris from the property. Buildings and Grounds Chairperson **Vince Beatty** will lead the effort on **April 7** beginning at **8:00 am**. There are a number of outdoor projects and improvements the Society has been waiting for favorable weather to perform. Stop by the museum for more information and to sign up. Clean grounds will ensure that the Clark House and Armory represent the town of Indiana in a positive light during the busy tour season that lies ahead.

Spring cleaning is not only taking place outdoors. The Society has been hard at work since the end of 2017 organizing one of its many collection storage areas. Material is being rehoused into proper containers and organized for easier access. The document room is nearing completion as the Society looks to finish installation of some much needed shelving. The Society would like to thank **Gary Clawson Jr.** for hauling the parts from Pittsburgh, saving the Society a significant sum on freight costs. Increased organization will give the Society greater intellectual control over its artifacts and archives, thus making them more accessible to the public.

Edna Todd Bell's Eight Generation Pedigree Chart

Edna Bell Pierce with her two oldest children @ 1923
Martha Elizabeth "Betty" Pierce
William Taylor "Bill" Pierce

To be born a Scot
Is to be born privileged.

You have music in your blood,
Courage in your heart,
And fire in your soul.

Scottish Naming Pattern

Being familiar with these patterns will allow you to make genealogical inferences, identify potential new avenues of research and reveal all sorts of clues about the lives of your ancestors. By the latter part of the nineteenth century, these patterns began to break down and fade out of use so be cautious when using them to identify more recent ancestors.

The traditional patterns used when naming boys were as follows:

The first son would be named after the father's father (variation is after the mother's father)
The second after the mother's father (variation is the father's father)
The third son would be named after the father
The fourth son would be named after the father's oldest brother (variation is after the father's paternal grandfather)
The fifth son would be named after the mother's oldest brother (variation is after the mother's paternal grandfather)

and for girls:

First daughter named after the mother's mother (variation is after the father's mother)
Second daughter named after the father's mother
Third daughter named after the mother
Fourth daughter named after the mother's oldest sister (variation is after the mother's maternal grandmother)
Fifth daughter named after the father's oldest sister (variation is after the father's maternal grandmother)

These formulas may come in handy when identifying potential members of your ancestor's immediate family. However, it's always worth bearing in mind that certain family circumstances could divert these patterns from their usual course. For example, you may find that certain given names were duplicated within the same generation. This could be the result of both grandfathers sharing a common name that was then given to two children, or, it could hint at the death of an earlier child within the family as it was not uncommon for parent's to name later children after dead siblings.

To make matters even more complicated, there was yet another set of patterns that used the names of ancestors rather than the parent's siblings. This "ancestral pattern" was outlined by U.S. family historian, John B Robb, in his 2012 paper; "The Scottish Onomastic Child-naming Pattern". According to Robb, the pattern for boys was as follows:

The first son was named for his father's father.
The second son was named for his mother's father.
The third son was named for his father's father's father.
The fourth son was named for his mother's mother's father.
The fifth son was named for his father's mother's father.
The sixth son was named for his mother's father's father.
The seventh through tenth sons were named for their father's four great-grandfathers.
The eleventh through fourteenth sons were named for their mother's four great-grandfathers.

and for girls:

The first daughter was named for her mother's mother.
The second daughter was named for her father's mother.
The third daughter was named for her mother's father's mother.
The fourth daughter was named for her father's father's mother.
The fifth daughter was named for her mother's mother's mother.
The sixth daughter was named for her father's mother's mother.
The seventh through tenth daughters were named for their mother's four great-grandmothers.
The eleventh through fourteenth daughters were named for their father's four great-grandmothers.

* Note – the page numbers at the bottom of the Edna Todd Bell Pedigree Chart do not correspond with the pages in this book. They do, however, correspond to the page numbers on the right side of the chart pages. This should enable you to navigate the chart hopefully without too much confusion.

Pedigree Chart for
Edna Todd Bell

Parents

Grandparents

Great-Grandparents

Joseph Bell
b: Jan 1796 in Sewickley
     Stlmt, Westmoreland Co, PA
m: 1825
d: 19 Jun 1860 in Perrysville,
     Jefferson Co., PA
2

Hugh McKee Bell
b: 11 Aug 1826 in Perrysville,
     Jefferson Co., PA
m: 22 Jul 1852 in Perrysville,
     Jefferson Co., PA
d: 23 Mar 1911 in Perrysville,
     Jefferson Co., PA

Sarah Thompson McKee
b: 1796 in Indiana Co., PA
d: 1833 in Perrysville,
     Jefferson Co., PA
3

John Taylor Bell
b: 16 Sep 1853 in Frostburg,
     Jefferson Co., PA
m: 15 Sep 1885
d: 18 Oct 1926 in Indiana,
     Indiana Co., PA

John Martin
b: 1799 in England
m: 27 Apr 1815
d: 08 Jul 1876 in Frostburg,
     Jefferson Co., PA
4

Eleanor "Ellen" Martin
b: 11 May 1825 in Perrysville,
     Jefferson Co., PA
d: 04 Apr 1911 in Perrysville,
     Jefferson Co., PA

Elizabeth Elder
b: 22 Nov 1788 in
     Pennsylvania, USA
d: 31 Aug 1852 in Frostburg,
     Jefferson Co., PA
5

Edna Todd Bell
b: 04 Oct 1890 in Indiana, PA
m: 17 Jan 1917 in Indiana, PA
d: 27 Jul 1973 in Indiana, PA

Hon. James Todd Jr
b: 22 Feb 1788 in Belfast,
     Ireland
m: 1808 in Pennsylvania
d: 18 Sep 1872 in Indiana,
     Indiana Co., PA
6

William A. Todd
b: 01 Aug 1825 in Indiana,
     Indiana Co., PA
m: 1851 in Pennsylvania
d: 03 Jan 1860 in Indiana,
     Indiana Co., PA

Elizabeth Mahaffey
b: 01 May 1787 in Indiana,
     Pennsylvania
d: 07 Sep 1842 in Indiana,
     Pennsylvania
7

Elizabeth Drum Todd
b: 05 Jun 1854 in Indiana,
     Indiana Co., PA
d: 04 Jun 1904 in Indiana,
     Indiana Co., PA

Henry Drum
b: 01 Jan 1796 in Greensburg,
     Westmoreland, Pennsylvania
m:
d: 12 Mar 1879 in Indiana,
     Indiana Co PA
8

Susan Drum
b: 22 Oct 1828 in Saltsburg,
     Indiana Co., PA
d: 28 Jul 1899 in Indiana,
     Indiana Co., PA

Margaret Charlotte McPherrin
b: 16 Jul 1796 in Welsh Run,
     Franklin, Pennsylvania
d: 1828 in Saltsburg, Indiana
     Co. PA
9

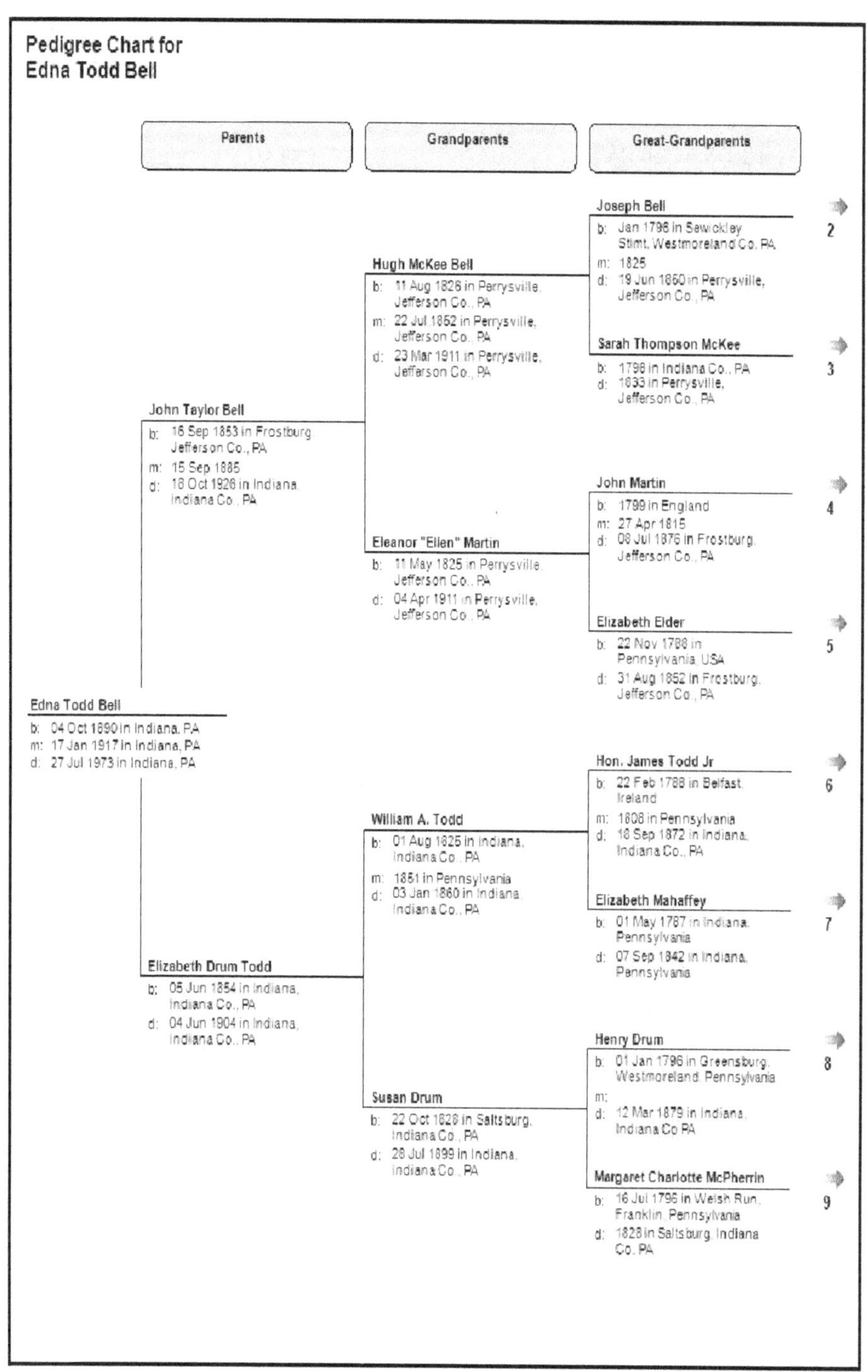

1

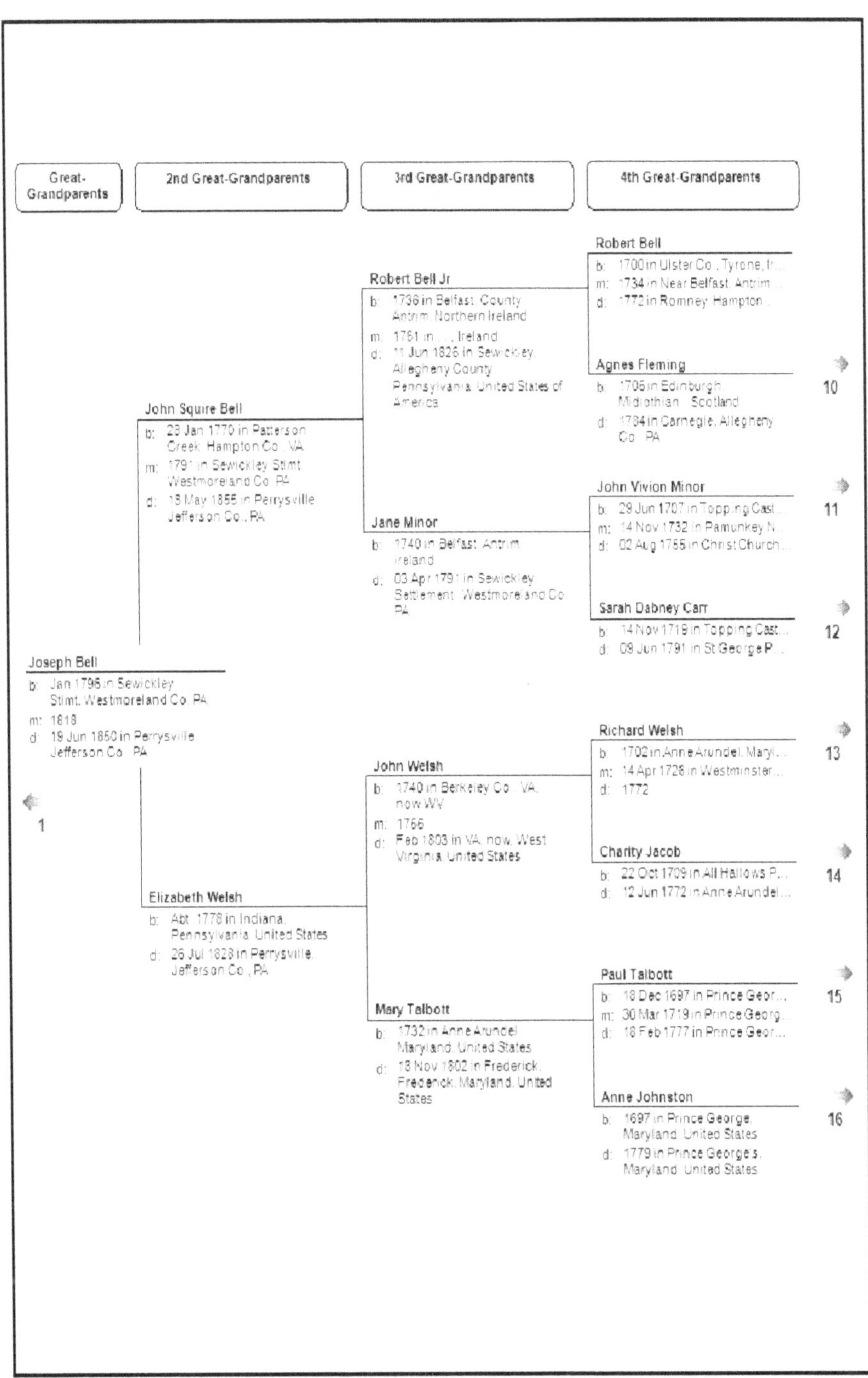

Great-Grandparents
2nd Great-Grandparents
3rd Great-Grandparents
4th Great-Grandparents

Robert Bell Jr
b: 1736 in Belfast, County Antrim, Northern Ireland
m: 1761 in ..., Ireland
d: 11 Jun 1826 in Sewickley, Allegheny County, Pennsylvania, United States of America

Robert Bell
b: 1700 in Ulster Co., Tyrone, Ir...
m: 1734 in Near Belfast, Antrim...
d: 1772 in Romney, Hampton...

Agnes Fleming
b: 1706 in Edinburgh, Midlothian, Scotland
d: 1784 in Carnegie, Allegheny Co., PA
10

John Squire Bell
b: 23 Jan 1770 in Patterson Creek, Hampton Co., VA
m: 1791 in Sewickley Stlmt, Westmoreland Co., PA
d: 18 May 1855 in Perrysville, Jefferson Co., PA

Jane Minor
b: 1740 in Belfast, Antrim, Ireland
d: 03 Apr 1791 in Sewickley Settlement, Westmoreland Co., PA

John Vivion Minor
b: 29 Jun 1707 in Topping Cast...
m: 14 Nov 1732 in Pamunkey N...
d: 02 Aug 1765 in Christ Church...
11

Sarah Dabney Carr
b: 14 Nov 1719 in Topping Cast...
d: 09 Jun 1791 in St. George P...
12

Joseph Bell
b: Jan 1798 in Sewickley Stlmt, Westmoreland Co., PA
m: 1818
d: 19 Jun 1850 in Perrysville, Jefferson Co., PA
1

John Welsh
b: 1740 in Berkeley Co., VA, now WV
m: 1766
d: Feb 1803 in VA, now West Virginia, United States

Richard Welsh
b: 1702 in Anne Arundel, Maryl...
m: 14 Apr 1728 in Westminster...
d: 1772
13

Charity Jacob
b: 22 Oct 1709 in All Hallows P...
d: 12 Jun 1772 in Anne Arundel...
14

Elizabeth Welsh
b: Abt. 1778 in Indiana, Pennsylvania, United States
d: 26 Jul 1828 in Perrysville, Jefferson Co., PA

Mary Talbott
b: 1732 in Anne Arundel, Maryland, United States
d: 18 Nov 1802 in Frederick, Frederick, Maryland, United States

Paul Talbott
b: 18 Dec 1697 in Prince Geor...
m: 30 Mar 1719 in Prince Georg...
d: 18 Feb 1777 in Prince Geor...
15

Anne Johnston
b: 1697 in Prince George, Maryland, United States
d: 1779 in Prince George's, Maryland, United States
16

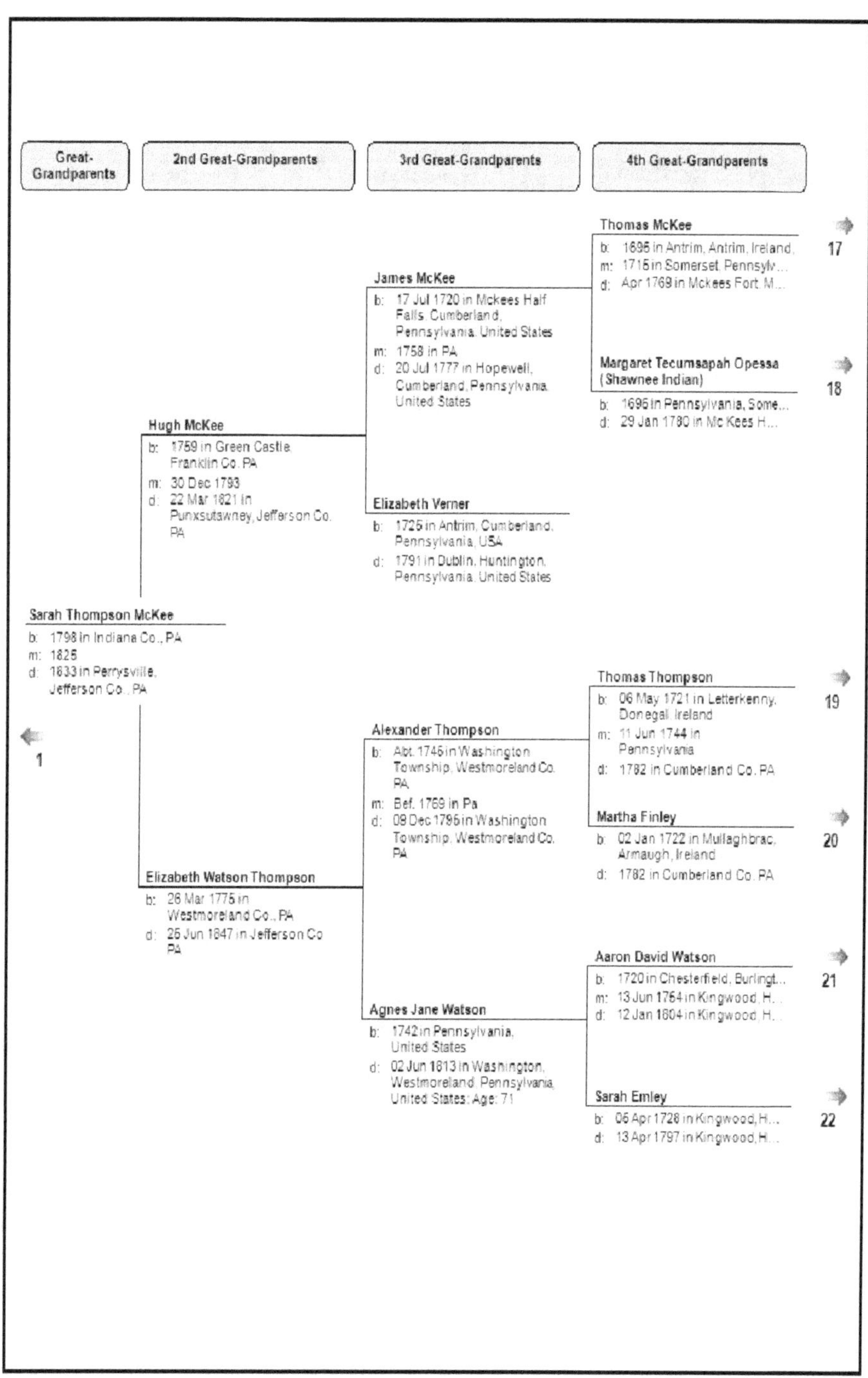

Great-Grandparents
2nd Great-Grandparents
3rd Great-Grandparents
4th Great-Grandparents

Thomas McKee
b: 1696 in Antrim, Antrim, Ireland,
m: 1715 in Somerset, Pennsylv...
d: Apr 1769 in Mckees Fort, M...
17

James McKee
b: 17 Jul 1720 in Mckees Half
     Falls, Cumberland,
     Pennsylvania, United States
m: 1758 in PA
d: 20 Jul 1777 in Hopewell,
     Cumberland, Pennsylvania,
     United States

Margaret Tecumsapah Opessa
(Shawnee Indian)
b: 1696 in Pennsylvania, Some...
d: 29 Jan 1780 in Mc Kees H...
18

Hugh McKee
b: 1759 in Green Castle,
     Franklin Co. PA
m: 30 Dec 1793
d: 22 Mar 1821 in
     Punxsutawney, Jefferson Co.
     PA

Elizabeth Verner
b: 1725 in Antrim, Cumberland,
     Pennsylvania, USA
d: 1791 in Dublin, Huntington,
     Pennsylvania, United States

Sarah Thompson McKee
b: 1798 in Indiana Co., PA
m: 1825
d: 1833 in Perrysville,
     Jefferson Co., PA
1

Thomas Thompson
b: 06 May 1721 in Letterkenny,
     Donegal, Ireland
m: 11 Jun 1744 in
     Pennsylvania
d: 1782 in Cumberland Co. PA
19

Alexander Thompson
b: Abt. 1746 in Washington
     Township, Westmoreland Co.
     PA
m: Bef. 1769 in Pa
d: 09 Dec 1795 in Washington
     Township, Westmoreland Co.
     PA

Martha Finley
b: 02 Jan 1722 in Mullaghbrac,
     Armaugh, Ireland
d: 1782 in Cumberland Co. PA
20

Elizabeth Watson Thompson
b: 26 Mar 1775 in
     Westmoreland Co., PA
d: 26 Jun 1847 in Jefferson Co
     PA

Aaron David Watson
b: 1720 in Chesterfield, Burlingt...
m: 13 Jun 1764 in Kingwood, H...
d: 12 Jan 1804 in Kingwood, H...
21

Agnes Jane Watson
b: 1742 in Pennsylvania,
     United States
d: 02 Jun 1813 in Washington,
     Westmoreland, Pennsylvania,
     United States; Age: 71

Sarah Emley
b: 06 Apr 1728 in Kingwood, H...
d: 13 Apr 1797 in Kingwood, H...
22

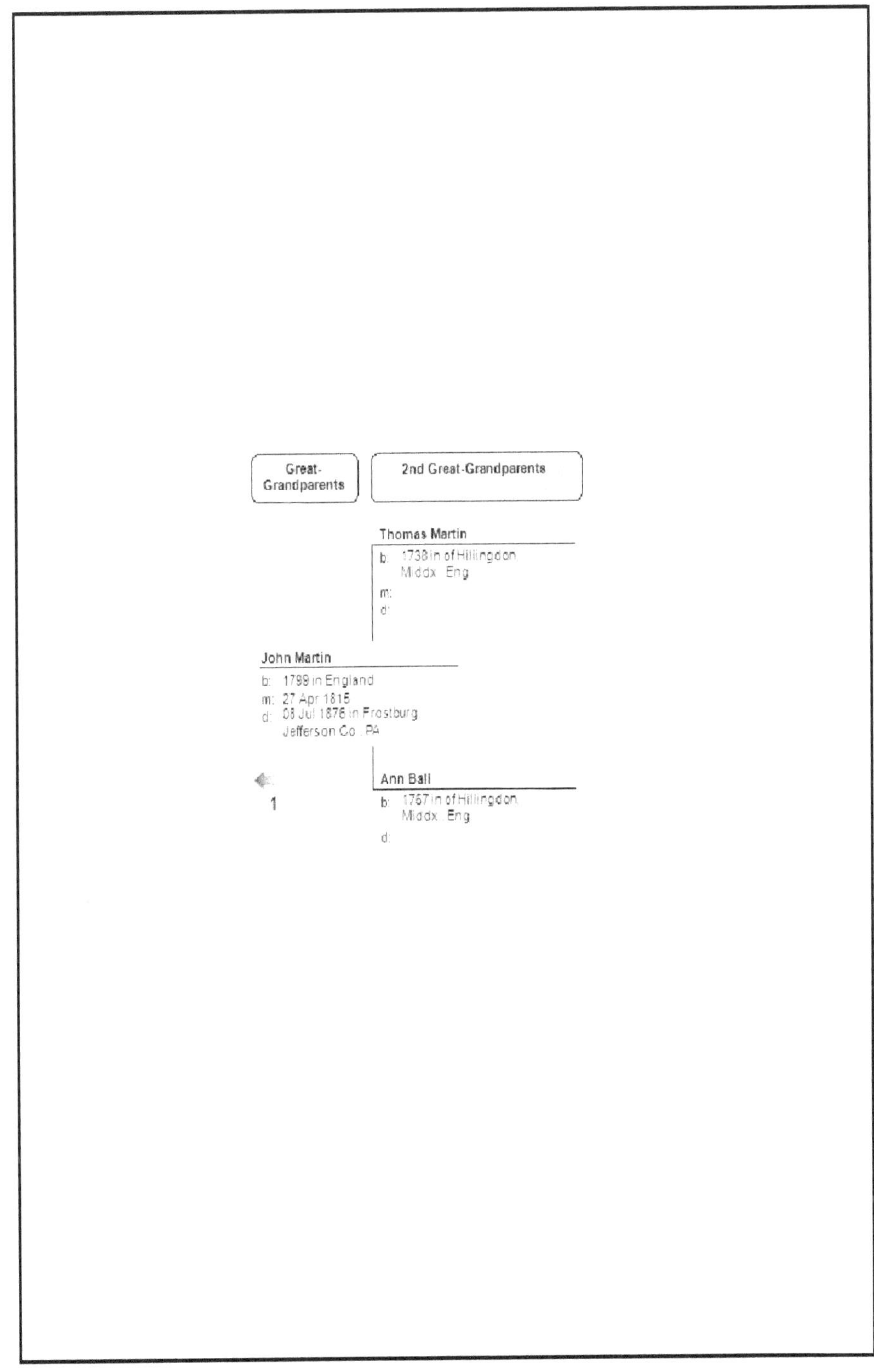

Great-Grandparents
2nd Great-Grandparents
Thomas Martin
b: 1738 in of Hillingdon
     Middx , Eng
m:
d:
John Martin
b: 1799 in England
m: 27 Apr 1815
d: 08 Jul 1876 in Frostburg
     Jefferson Co , PA
1
Ann Ball
b: 1767 in of Hillingdon
     Middx , Eng
d:

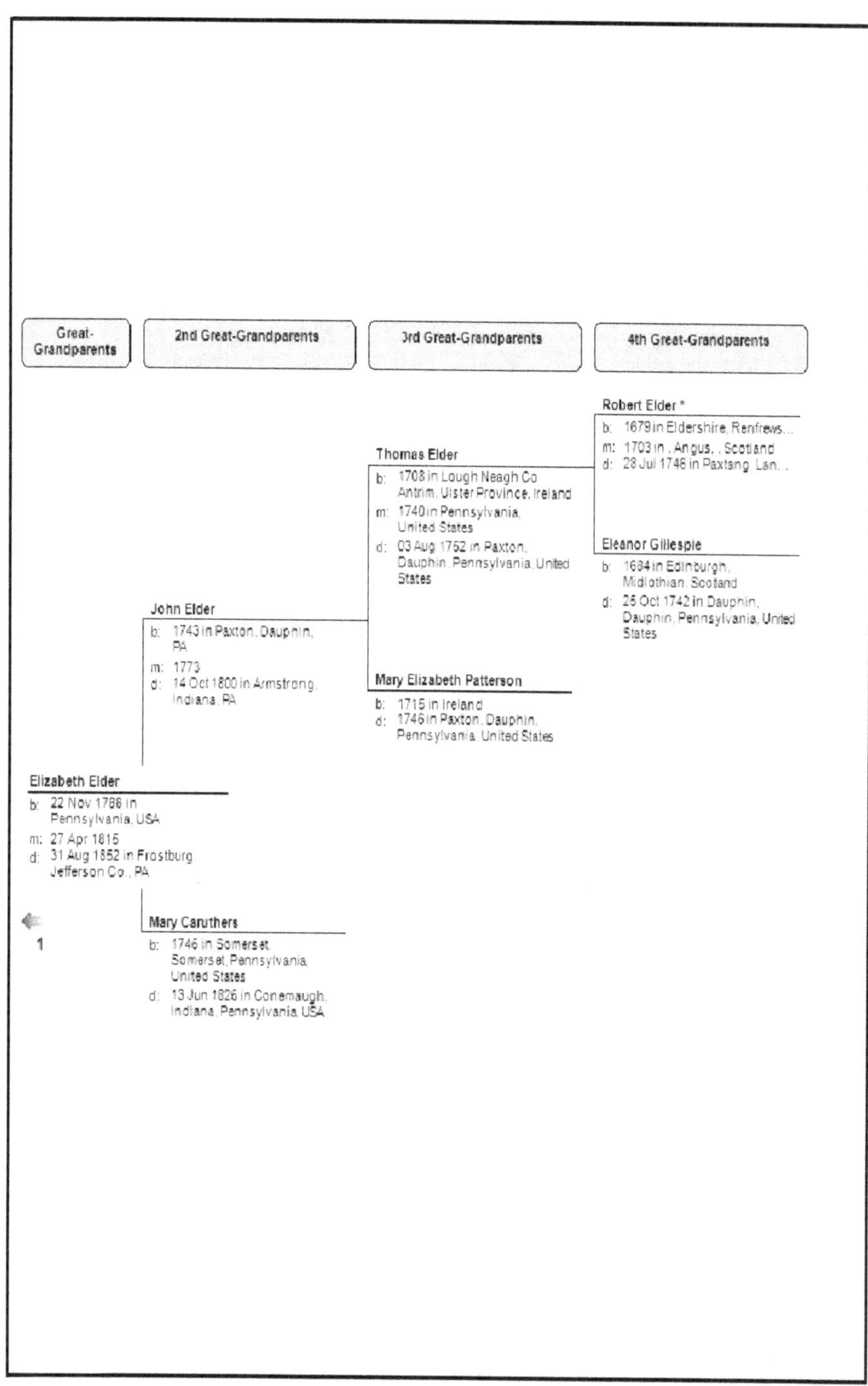

Great-Grandparents
2nd Great-Grandparents
3rd Great-Grandparents
4th Great-Grandparents

Robert Elder *
b: 1679 in Eldershire, Renfrews...
m: 1703 in , Angus, , Scotland
d: 28 Jul 1746 in Paxtang, Lan...

Thomas Elder
b: 1708 in Lough Neagh Co Antrim, Ulster Province, Ireland
m: 1740 in Pennsylvania, United States
d: 03 Aug 1752 in Paxton, Dauphin, Pennsylvania, United States

Eleanor Gillespie
b: 1684 in Edinburgh, Midlothian, Scotland
d: 25 Oct 1742 in Dauphin, Dauphin, Pennsylvania, United States

John Elder
b: 1743 in Paxton, Dauphin, PA
m: 1773
d: 14 Oct 1800 in Armstrong, Indiana, PA

Mary Elizabeth Patterson
b: 1715 in Ireland
d: 1746 in Paxton, Dauphin, Pennsylvania, United States

Elizabeth Elder
b: 22 Nov 1786 in Pennsylvania, USA
m: 27 Apr 1815
d: 31 Aug 1852 in Frostburg Jefferson Co., PA

1

Mary Caruthers
b: 1746 in Somerset, Somerset, Pennsylvania, United States
d: 13 Jun 1826 in Conemaugh, Indiana, Pennsylvania, USA

Great-Grandparents
2nd Great-Grandparents

James Todd
b: 1769 in Of Belfast, Ireland
m: Bef. 1768 in Ireland
d: 1789 in Franklin Co near Chambersburg

Hon. James Todd Jr
b: 22 Feb 1788 in Belfast, Ireland
m: 1808 in Pennsylvania
d: 18 Sep 1872 in Indiana Indiana Co., PA

1

Mary Spence
b: 1765 in Ireland, United Kingdom
d: 18 Sep 1872 in Westmoreland Co., PA

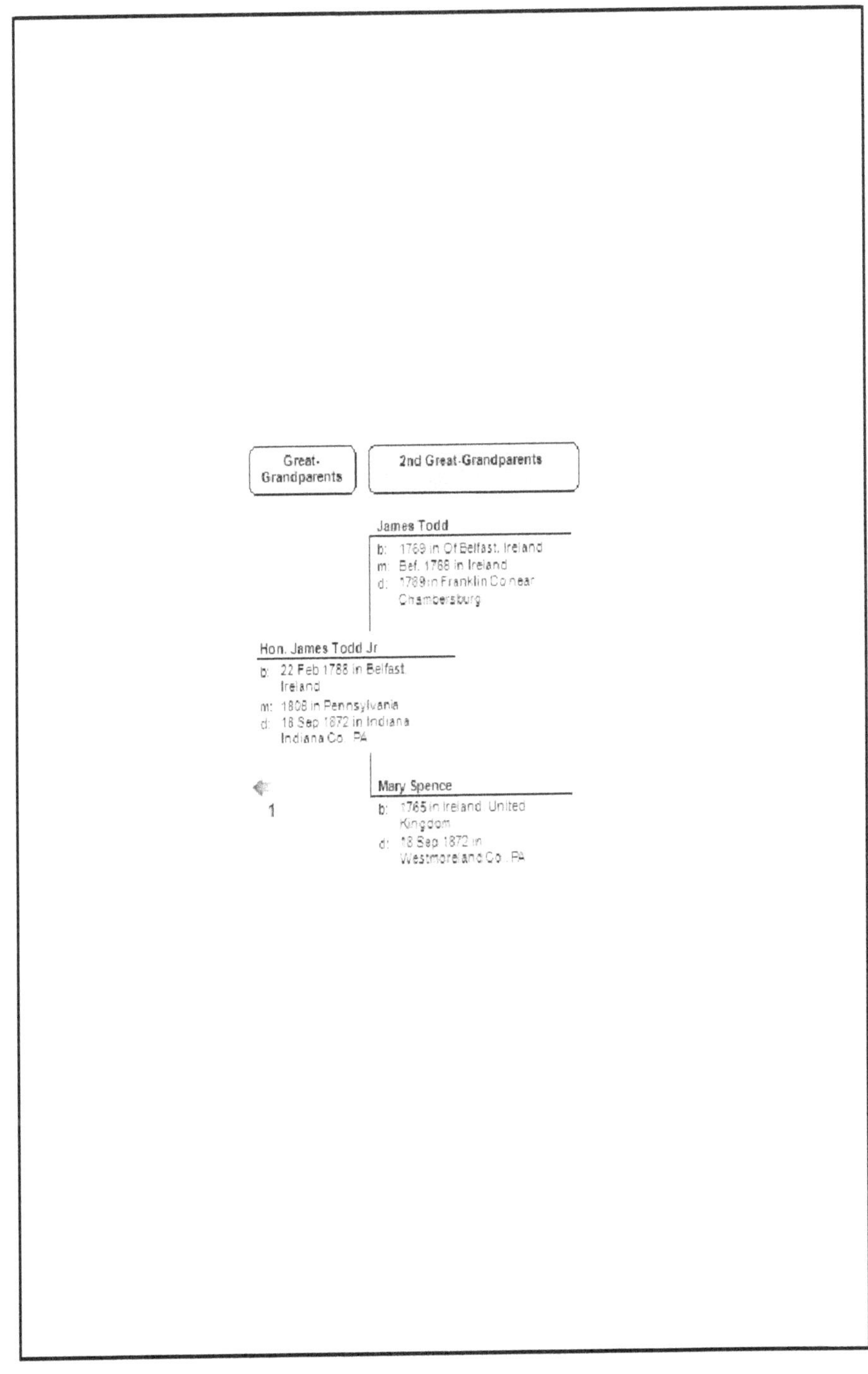

81

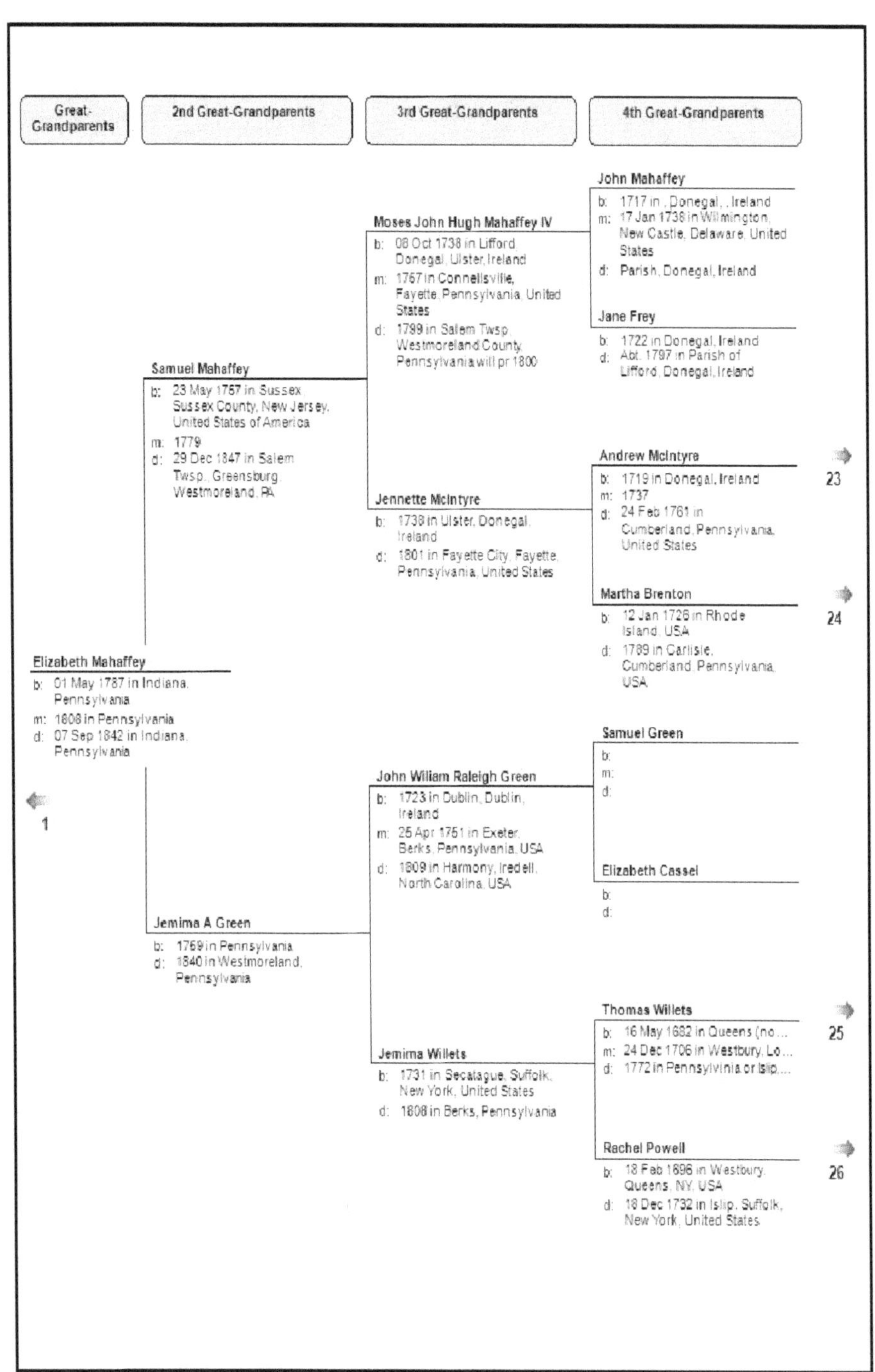

Great-Grandparents
2nd Great-Grandparents
3rd Great-Grandparents
4th Great-Grandparents

John Mahaffey
b: 1717 in , Donegal, , Ireland
m: 17 Jan 1738 in Wilmington, New Castle, Delaware, United States
d: Parish, Donegal, Ireland

Moses John Hugh Mahaffey IV
b: 08 Oct 1738 in Lifford, Donegal, Ulster, Ireland
m: 1767 in Connellsville, Fayette, Pennsylvania, United States
d: 1789 in Salem Twsp, Westmoreland County, Pennsylvania will pr 1800

Jane Frey
b: 1722 in Donegal, Ireland
d: Abt. 1797 in Parish of Lifford, Donegal, Ireland

Samuel Mahaffey
b: 23 May 1757 in Sussex, Sussex County, New Jersey, United States of America
m: 1779
d: 29 Dec 1847 in Salem Twsp., Greensburg, Westmoreland, PA

Andrew McIntyre
b: 1719 in Donegal, Ireland
m: 1737
d: 24 Feb 1761 in Cumberland, Pennsylvania, United States
23

Jennette McIntyre
b: 1738 in Ulster, Donegal, Ireland
d: 1801 in Fayette City, Fayette, Pennsylvania, United States

Martha Brenton
b: 12 Jan 1726 in Rhode Island, USA
d: 1789 in Carlisle, Cumberland, Pennsylvania, USA
24

Elizabeth Mahaffey
b: 01 May 1787 in Indiana, Pennsylvania
m: 1808 in Pennsylvania
d: 07 Sep 1842 in Indiana, Pennsylvania

Samuel Green
b:
m:
d:

John William Raleigh Green
b: 1723 in Dublin, Dublin, Ireland
m: 25 Apr 1751 in Exeter, Berks, Pennsylvania, USA
d: 1809 in Harmony, Iredell, North Carolina, USA

Elizabeth Cassel
b:
d:

1

Jemima A Green
b: 1769 in Pennsylvania
d: 1840 in Westmoreland, Pennsylvania

Thomas Willets
b: 16 May 1682 in Queens (no...
m: 24 Dec 1706 in Westbury, Lo...
d: 1772 in Pennsylvinia or Islip....
25

Jemima Willets
b: 1731 in Secatague, Suffolk, New York, United States
d: 1808 in Berks, Pennsylvania

Rachel Powell
b: 18 Feb 1696 in Westbury, Queens, NY, USA
d: 18 Dec 1732 in Islip, Suffolk, New York, United States
26

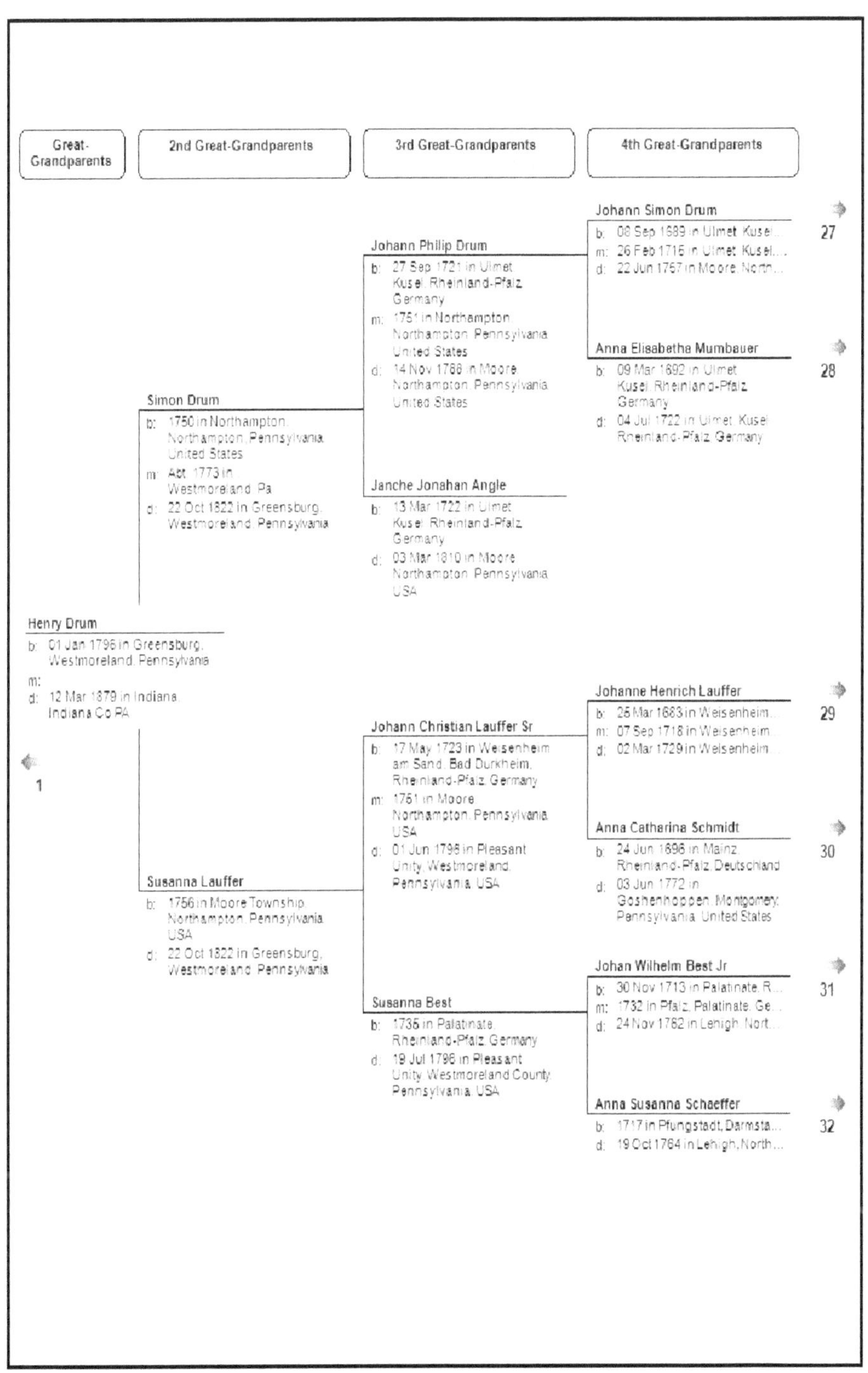

8

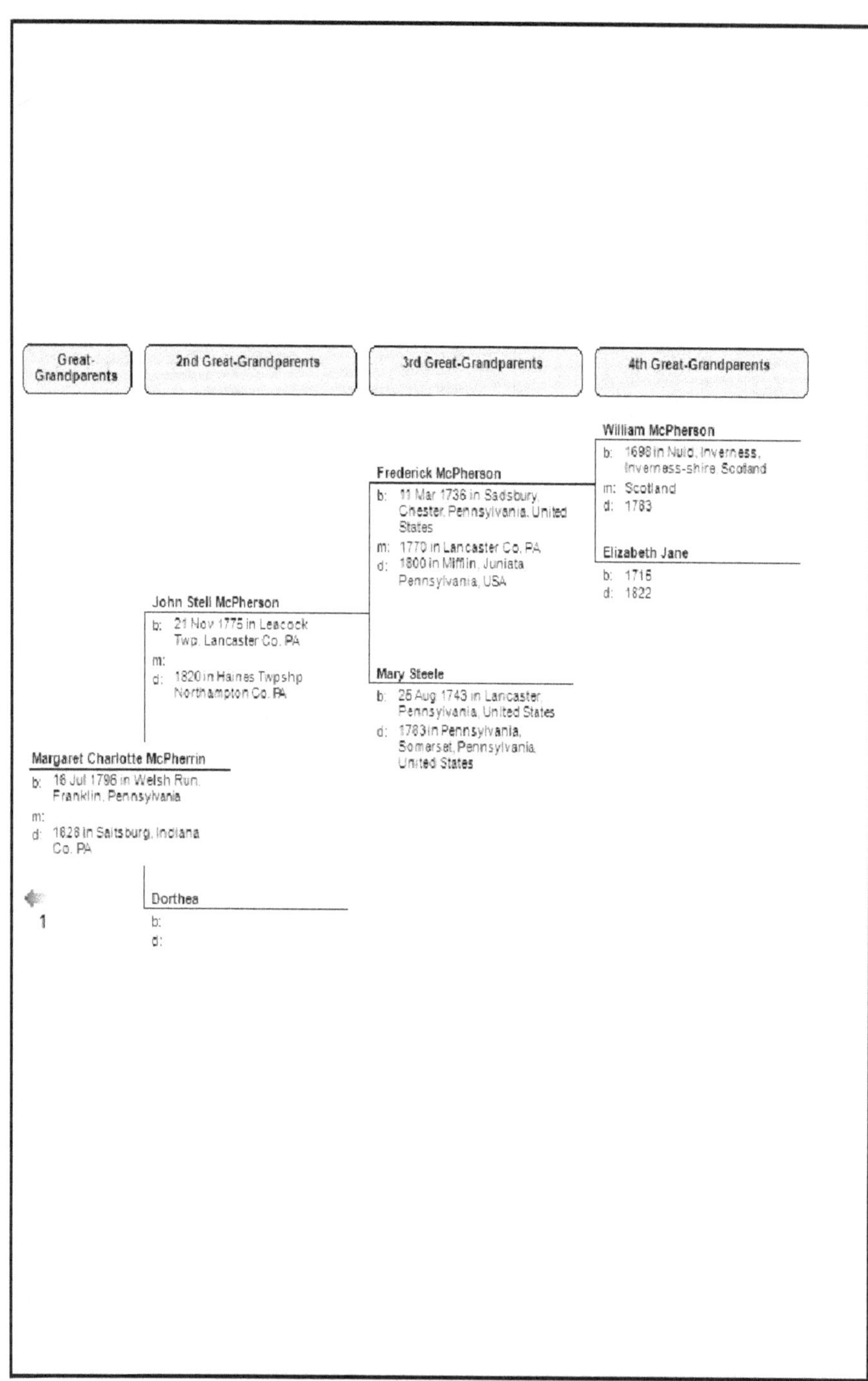

Great-Grandparents
2nd Great-Grandparents
3rd Great-Grandparents
4th Great-Grandparents

William McPherson
b: 1698 in Nuid, Inverness, Inverness-shire, Scotland
m: Scotland
d: 1783

Frederick McPherson
b: 11 Mar 1736 in Sadsbury, Chester, Pennsylvania, United States
m: 1770 in Lancaster Co, PA
d: 1800 in Mifflin, Juniata, Pennsylvania, USA

Elizabeth Jane
b: 1715
d: 1822

John Stell McPherson
b: 21 Nov 1775 in Leacock Twp, Lancaster Co, PA
m:
d: 1820 in Haines Twpshp Northampton Co, PA

Mary Steele
b: 25 Aug 1743 in Lancaster, Pennsylvania, United States
d: 1783 in Pennsylvania, Somerset, Pennsylvania, United States

Margaret Charlotte McPherrin
b: 16 Jul 1796 in Welsh Run, Franklin, Pennsylvania
m:
d: 1828 in Saltsburg, Indiana Co, PA

1

Dorthea
b:
d:

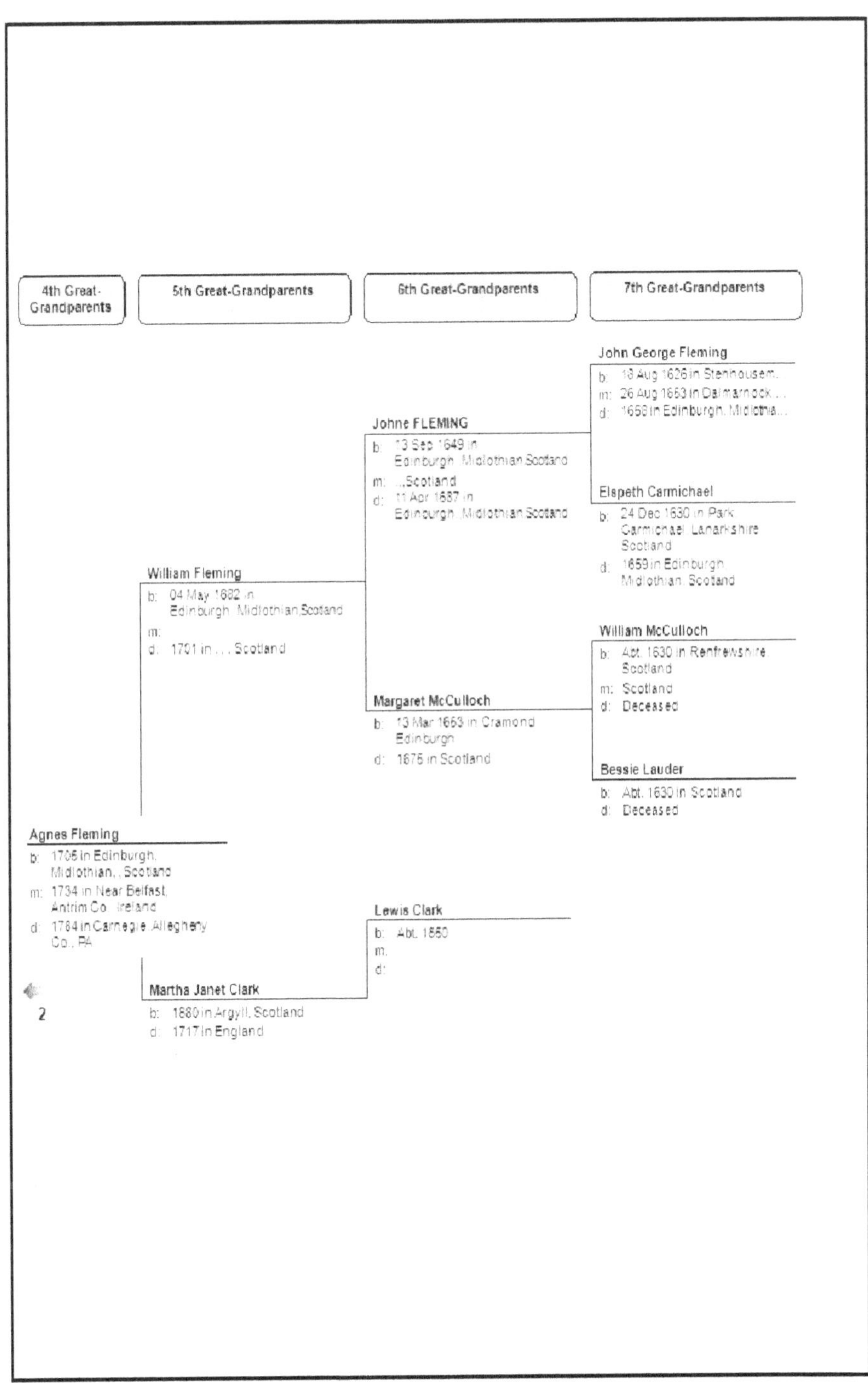

4th Great-Grandparents

5th Great-Grandparents

6th Great-Grandparents

7th Great-Grandparents

John George Fleming
b: 18 Aug 1626 in Stenhousem...
m: 26 Aug 1663 in Dalmarnock ...
d: 1658 in Edinburgh, Midlothia...

Johne FLEMING
b: 13 Sep 1649 in
Edinburgh, Midlothian Scotland
m: ..Scotland
d: 11 Apr 1687 in
Edinburgh, Midlothian Scotland

Elspeth Carmichael
b: 24 Dec 1630 in Park,
Carmichael, Lanarkshire
Scotland
d: 1659 in Edinburgh,
Midlothian, Scotland

William Fleming
b: 04 May 1682 in
Edinburgh, Midlothian,Scotland
m:
d: 1701 in . . , Scotland

William McCulloch
b: Abt. 1630 in Renfrewshire
Scotland
m: Scotland
d: Deceased

Margaret McCulloch
b: 13 Mar 1663 in Cramond
Edinburgh
d: 1675 in Scotland

Bessie Lauder
b: Abt. 1630 in Scotland
d: Deceased

Agnes Fleming
b: 1705 in Edinburgh,
Midlothian,..Scotland
m: 1734 in Near Belfast,
Antrim Co. Ireland
d: 1784 in Carnegie, Allegheny
Co., PA

Lewis Clark
b: Abt. 1650
m:
d:

2

Martha Janet Clark
b: 1680 in Argyll, Scotland
d: 1717 in England

85

4th Great-Grandparents

5th Great-Grandparents

6th Great-Grandparents

7th Great-Grandparents

Meindert Doodes Minor II
b: 1640 in Topping Castle, Caroline, Virginia, United States
m: VA
d: 13 Nov 1894 in Middlesex, Virginia, USA

Captain Meindert (Maindort Minor Minert Meijnert) Geret Doodes (Doedes) Changed name to Minor after naturalization
b: 1621 in Holland, Reusel-de...
m: 1640 in Middlesex, Virginia...

Mary Guerat Johnson
b: May 1624 in Tiel, Gelderland, Netherlands
d: 09 Jan 1688 in Montague's Island, Middlesex, Virginia, USA

Garrett Minor
b: 13 Apr 1679 in Christ Church Parish, Middlesex Co., Virginia, USA
m: 17 Oct 1706 in Middlesex, Virginia, United States
d: 02 Feb 1720 in Christ Church Parish, Middlesex Co., Virginia, USA

Elizabeth Cocke(Montague)
b: Abt. 1838 in Bremo, Henrico, Virginia, United States
d: 1708 in Christ Church, Middlesex, Virginia, United States

Richard Cocke
b: 06 Sep 1602 in Stottesden...
m: 1652 in Bremo, Henrico, Vir...
d: 04 Oct 1665 in Bremo, Henri...

Mary Aston Clark
b: 21 Feb 1608 in Charles City, Charles, Virginia colony, America
d: 1693 in Charles City, Charles, Virginia, United States

John Vivion Minor
b: 29 Jun 1707 in Topping Castle, Caroline, Virginia, United States
m: 14 Nov 1732 in Pamunkey Neck, King William, Virginia, United States
d: 02 Aug 1755 in Christ Church, Middlesex, Colony of Virginia

2

John Vivion
b: 1655 in Middlesex, Virginia, United States
m: Abt. 1676 in Christ Church Parish, Middlesex, Virginia, United States
d: 04 Jun 1705 in Saluda, Middlesex County, Virginia, USA

Thomas Vivion
b: 1635 in St Columb Major, C...
m: 1652 in Charles City County...
d: 1670 in Isle Wight, Virginia...

Mary A Owin
b: 22 Feb 1636 in Charles City, Charles, Virginia, United States
d: 1700 in Virginia, United States

Diana Vivion
b: 1680 in Middlesex, Virginia, United States
d: 16 Apr 1718 in Christ Church, Middlesex, Virginia, United States

Margaret Jane Smith
b: 25 Sep 1658 in Middlesex, Virginia, United States
d: 23 Feb 1704 in Middlesex, Virginia, United States

John Alexander Smith
b: 1631 in Bristol, Somerset,...
m: 1653 in Lancaster, Virginia...
d: 06 Apr 1696 in Middlesex, Vi...

Mary Anne Cocke
b: 1635 in Burton, Yorkshire,, England
d: 1657 in Middlesex, Virginia, United States. Arrived in 1653

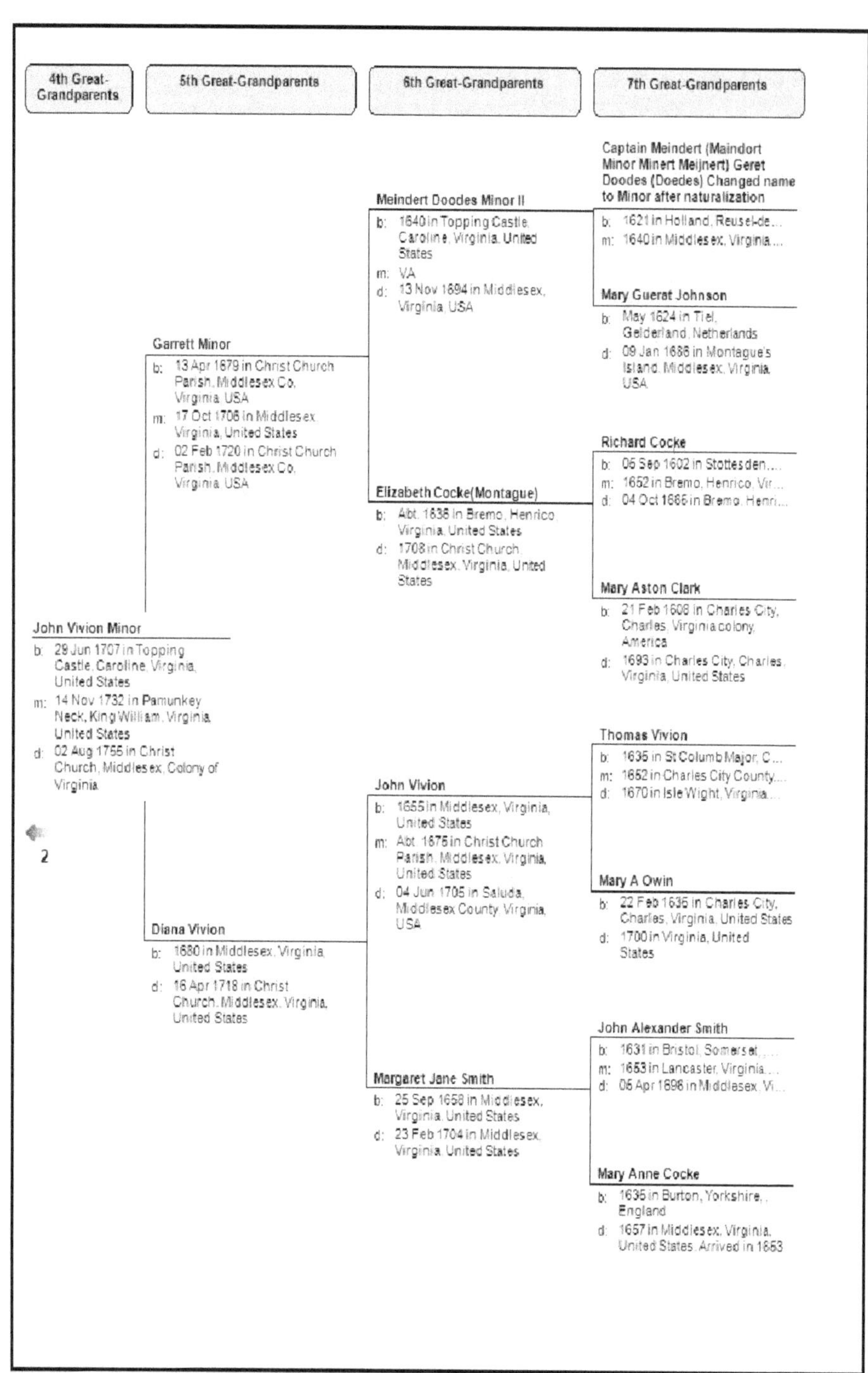

11

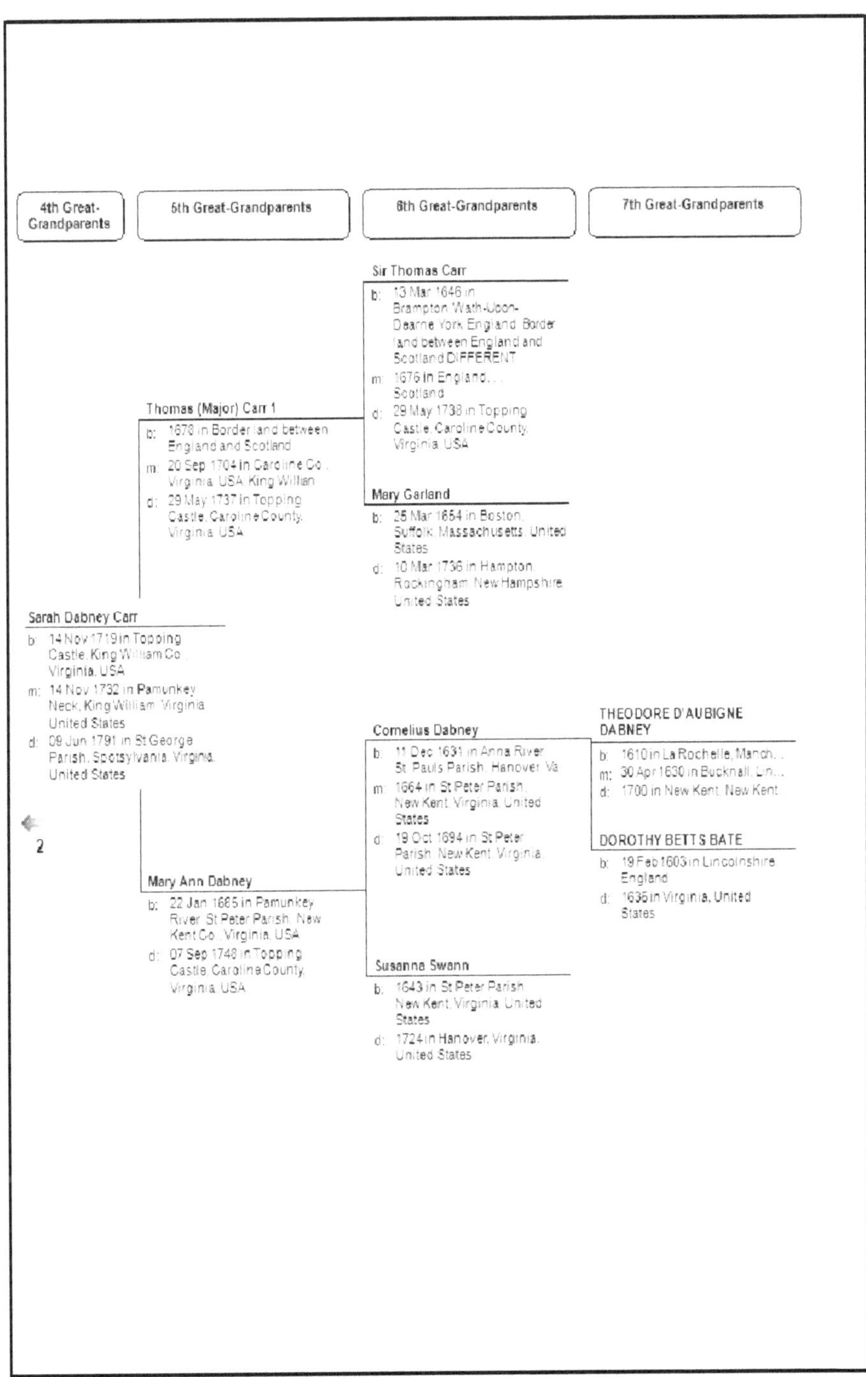

4th Great-Grandparents

5th Great-Grandparents

6th Great-Grandparents

7th Great-Grandparents

Sir Thomas Carr
b: 13 Mar 1646 in
    Brampton Wath-Upon-
    Dearne, York, England Border
    land between England and
    Scotland DIFFERENT
m: 1676 in England . . .
    Scotland
d: 29 May 1738 in Topping
    Castle, Caroline County,
    Virginia USA

Thomas (Major) Carr 1
b: 1678 in Border land between
    England and Scotland
m: 20 Sep 1704 in Caroline Co.,
    Virginia, USA King William
d: 29 May 1737 in Topping
    Castle, Caroline County,
    Virginia USA

Mary Garland
b: 25 Mar 1654 in Boston,
    Suffolk, Massachusetts, United
    States
d: 10 Mar 1736 in Hampton,
    Rockingham, New Hampshire,
    United States

Sarah Dabney Carr
b: 14 Nov 1719 in Topping
    Castle, King William Co.,
    Virginia, USA
m: 14 Nov 1732 in Pamunkey
    Neck, King William, Virginia,
    United States
d: 09 Jun 1791 in St George
    Parish, Spotsylvania, Virginia,
    United States

2

Cornelius Dabney
b: 11 Dec 1631 in Anna River,
    St. Pauls Parish, Hanover, Va
m: 1664 in St Peter Parish,
    New Kent, Virginia, United
    States
d: 19 Oct 1694 in St Peter
    Parish, New Kent, Virginia,
    United States

THEODORE D'AUBIGNE
DABNEY
b: 1610 in La Rochelle, Manch. . .
m: 30 Apr 1630 in Bucknall, Lin. . .
d: 1700 in New Kent, New Kent. . .

DOROTHY BETTS BATE
b: 19 Feb 1603 in Lincolnshire,
    England
d: 1635 in Virginia, United
    States

Mary Ann Dabney
b: 22 Jan 1665 in Pamunkey
    River, St Peter Parish, New
    Kent Co., Virginia, USA
d: 07 Sep 1748 in Topping
    Castle, Caroline County,
    Virginia USA

Susanna Swann
b: 1643 in St Peter Parish,
    New Kent, Virginia, United
    States
d: 1724 in Hanover, Virginia,
    United States

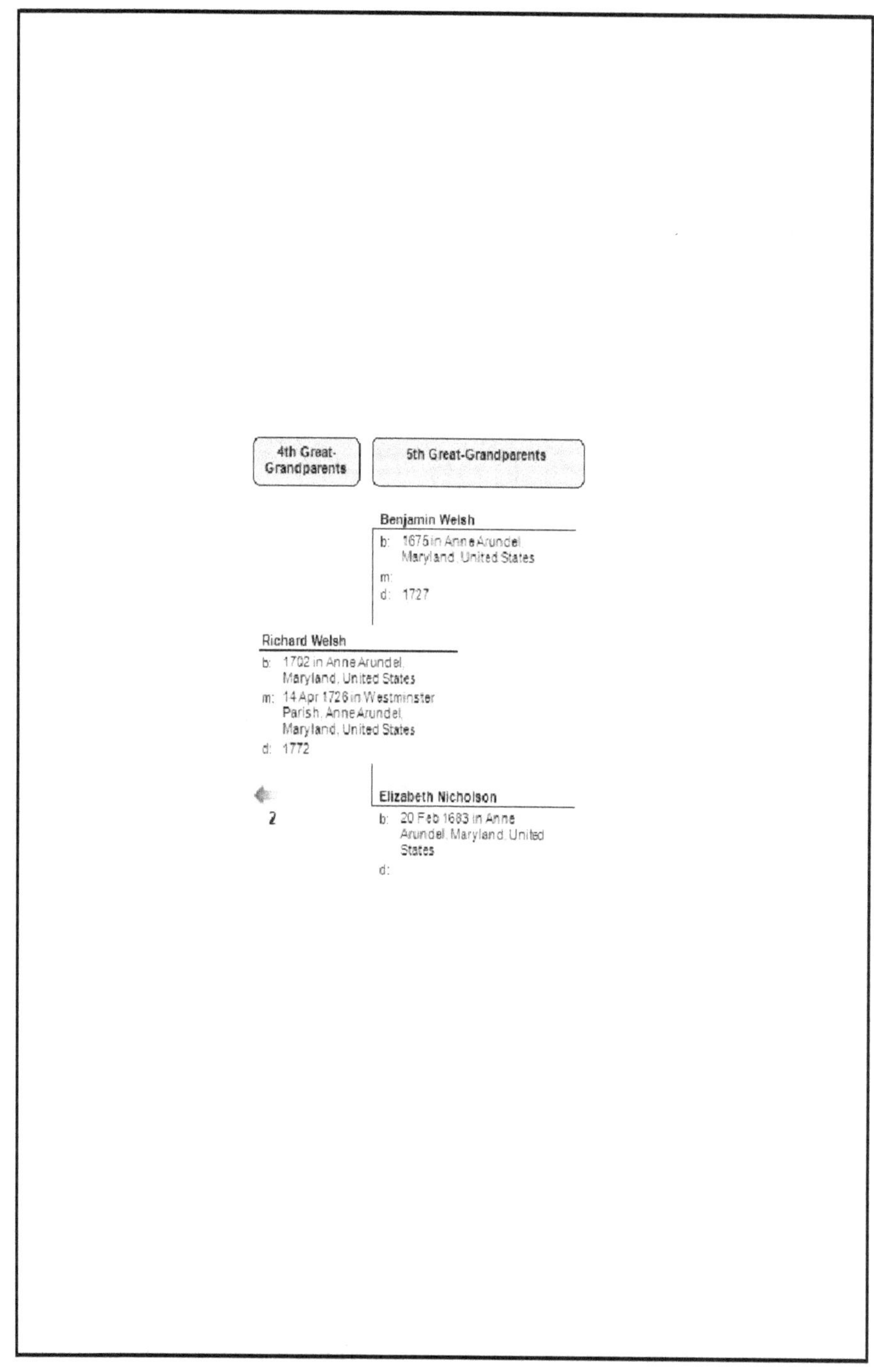

4th Great-Grandparents

5th Great-Grandparents

Benjamin Welsh
b: 1676 in Anne Arundel,
Maryland, United States
m:
d: 1727

Richard Welsh
b: 1702 in Anne Arundel,
Maryland, United States
m: 14 Apr 1726 in Westminster
Parish, Anne Arundel,
Maryland, United States
d: 1772

2

Elizabeth Nicholson
b: 20 Feb 1683 in Anne
Arundel, Maryland, United
States
d:

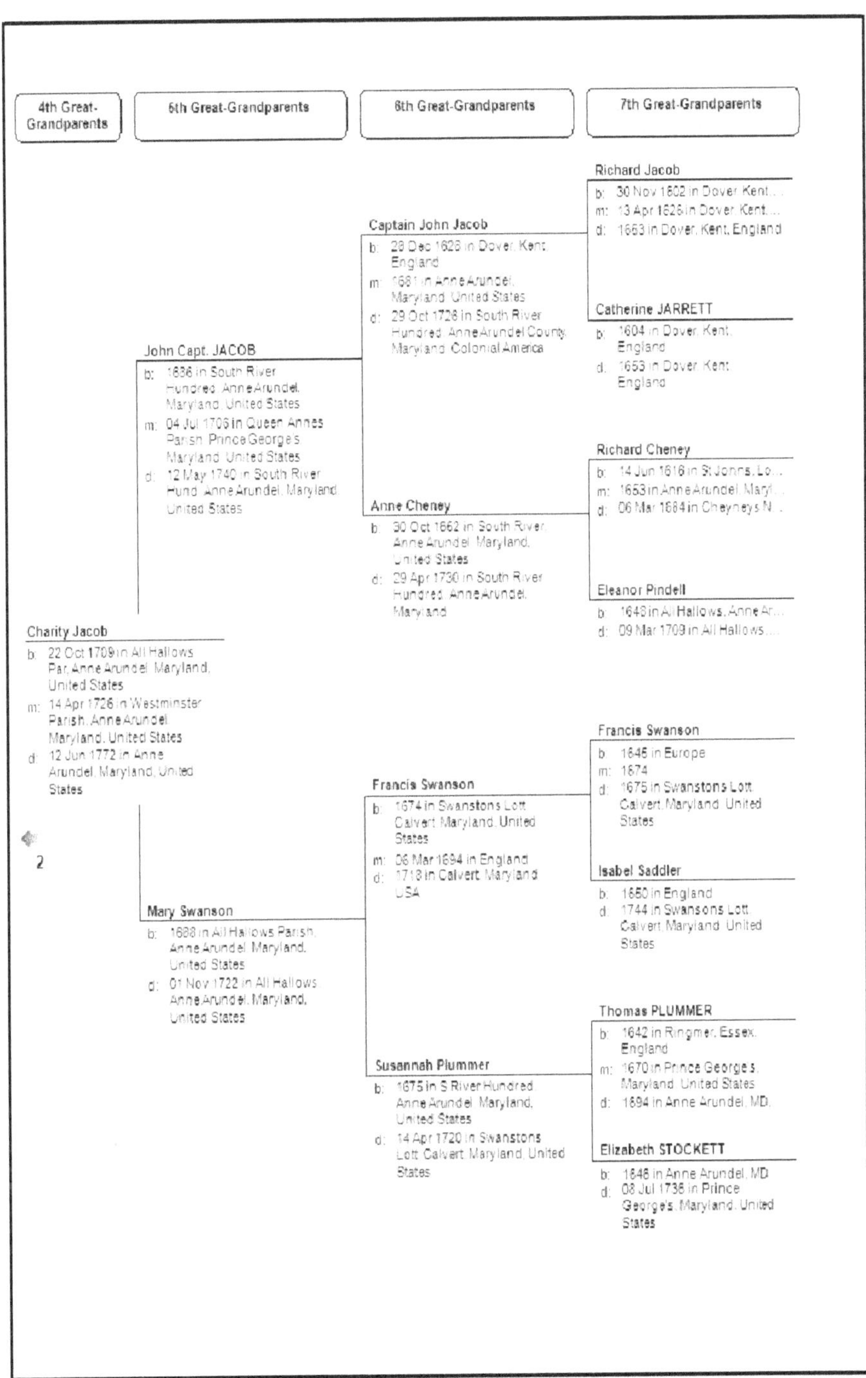

4th Great-Grandparents

6th Great-Grandparents

6th Great-Grandparents

7th Great-Grandparents

Richard Jacob
b: 30 Nov 1602 in Dover, Kent...
m: 13 Apr 1626 in Dover, Kent...
d: 1653 in Dover, Kent, England

Captain John Jacob
b: 28 Dec 1626 in Dover, Kent,
     England
m: 1681 in Anne Arundel,
     Maryland, United States
d: 29 Oct 1728 in South River
     Hundred, Anne Arundel County,
     Maryland, Colonial America

Catherine JARRETT
b: 1604 in Dover, Kent,
     England
d: 1653 in Dover, Kent,
     England

John Capt. JACOB
b: 1686 in South River
     Hundred, Anne Arundel,
     Maryland, United States
m: 04 Jul 1706 in Queen Annes
     Parish, Prince Georges,
     Maryland, United States
d: 12 May 1740 in South River
     Hund, Anne Arundel, Maryland,
     United States

Richard Cheney
b: 14 Jun 1616 in St Johns, Lo...
m: 1653 in Anne Arundel, Maryl...
d: 06 Mar 1684 in Cheyneys N...

Anne Cheney
b: 30 Oct 1662 in South River
     Anne Arundel, Maryland,
     United States
d: 29 Apr 1730 in South River
     Hundred, Anne Arundel,
     Maryland

Eleanor Pindell
b: 1648 in All Hallows, Anne Ar...
d: 09 Mar 1709 in All Hallows ...

Charity Jacob
b: 22 Oct 1709 in All Hallows
     Par, Anne Arundel, Maryland,
     United States
m: 14 Apr 1726 in Westminster
     Parish, Anne Arundel,
     Maryland, United States
d: 12 Jun 1772 in Anne
     Arundel, Maryland, United
     States

Francis Swanson
b: 1646 in Europe
m: 1674
d: 1675 in Swanstons Lott,
     Calvert, Maryland, United
     States

Francis Swanson
b: 1674 in Swanstons Lott,
     Calvert, Maryland, United
     States
m: 06 Mar 1694 in England
d: 1713 in Calvert, Maryland,
     USA

Isabel Saddler
b: 1650 in England
d: 1744 in Swansons Lott,
     Calvert, Maryland, United
     States

Mary Swanson
b: 1688 in All Hallows Parish,
     Anne Arundel, Maryland,
     United States
d: 01 Nov 1722 in All Hallows
     Anne Arundel, Maryland,
     United States

Thomas PLUMMER
b: 1642 in Ringmer, Essex,
     England
m: 1670 in Prince Georges,
     Maryland, United States
d: 1694 in Anne Arundel, MD.

Susannah Plummer
b: 1675 in S River Hundred,
     Anne Arundel, Maryland,
     United States
d: 14 Apr 1720 in Swanstons
     Lott, Calvert, Maryland, United
     States

Elizabeth STOCKETT
b: 1648 in Anne Arundel, MD.
d: 08 Jul 1736 in Prince
     Georges, Maryland, United
     States

2

14

Robert Talbot
b: 1600 in Waplington, Yorkshire, England
m: 1626
d: 22 May 1648 in Allerthorpe, Yorkshire, England

Paul Talbot
b: 29 Jan 1640 in Pocklington., Yorkshire England
m: 1676 in Romania
d: 04 Nov 1714 in Allerthorpe, Yorkshire, England

Ellis White
b: 1620 in Yorkshire, England
d: 26 May 1646 in England

John Talbot
b: 1671 in Pocklington, Yorkshire, England
m: 02 Feb 1696 in Piscataway, Prince George's, Maryland, United States
d: 26 May 1735 in Piscataway, Prince George's, Maryland, United States

Cordelia Anne Hewes
b: 1649 in Romania
d: 1760 in Maryland, United States

Paul Talbott
b: 18 Dec 1697 in Prince George's, Maryland, United States
m: 30 Mar 1719 in Prince George's, Maryland, United States
d: 18 Feb 1777 in Prince George's, Maryland, United States

Thomas Lockyear
b: 1620
m:
d: 1660 in Milton, Kent, England

Thomas Lockyear
b: 1650 in Milton, Kent, England
m: 1659 in MD
d: 16 May 1722 in Piscataway, Prince George's, Maryland, United States

Elizabeth Jarrett
b: 1620 in Ottery St Mary, Devon, England
d: 1671 in Britford, Wiltshire, England

Sarah Lockyear
b: 1676 in Prince George's, Maryland, United States
d: 1762 in Fort Washington, Prince George's, Maryland, United States

John Anthony Johnson Jr
b: 07 Feb 1640 in Lincolnshire...
m: 02 Dec 1660 in St Mary, W...
d: 09 Feb 1702 in Dunstan, St...

Elizabeth Johnson
b: 28 Mar 1662 in Milton, Kent, England
d: 16 May 1722 in Piscataway, Prince George's, Maryland, United States

Mary Hardine
b: 1640 in Spondon, Derbyshire, England
d: 26 Jun 1674 in Derby, Derbyshire, England

2

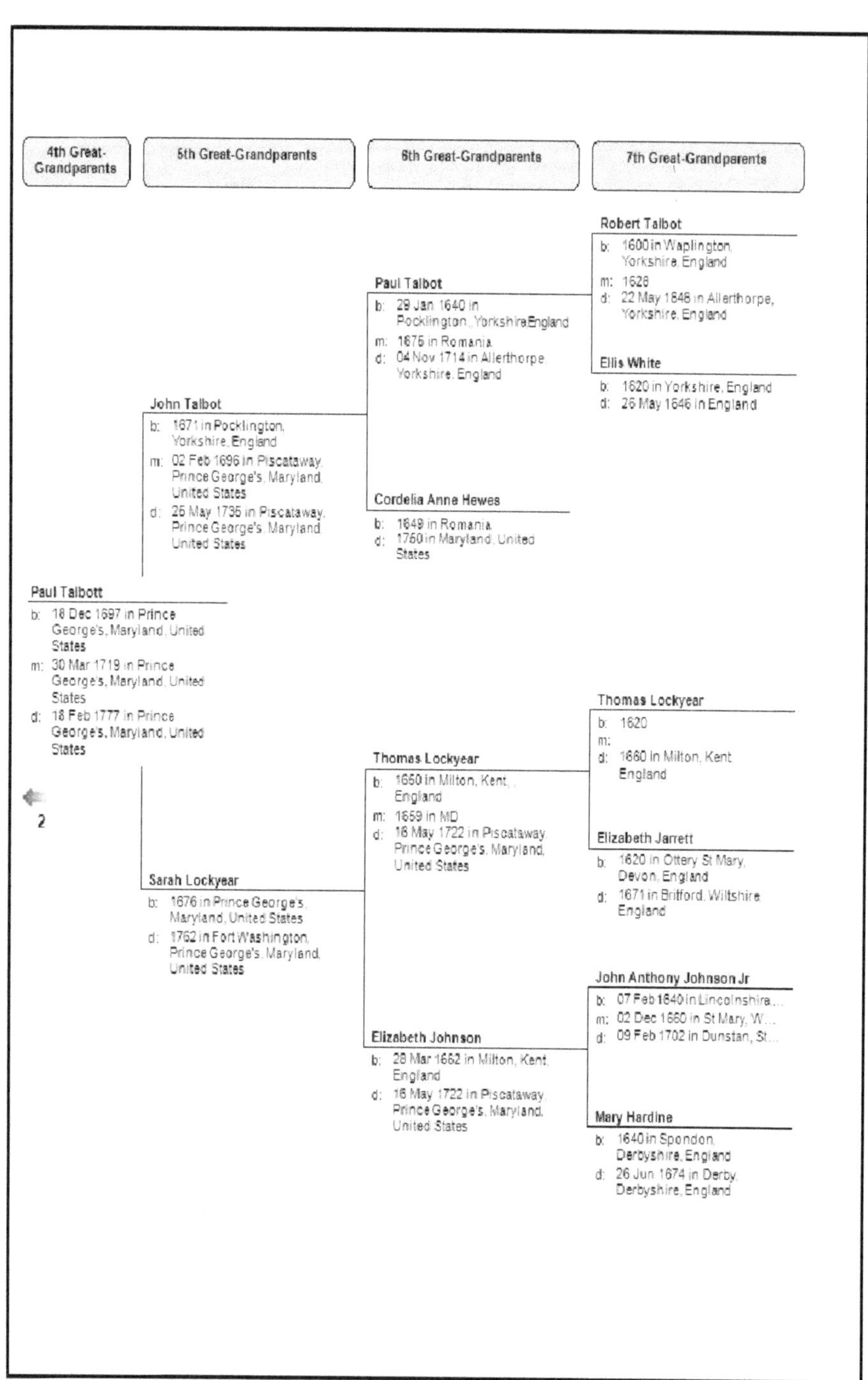

15

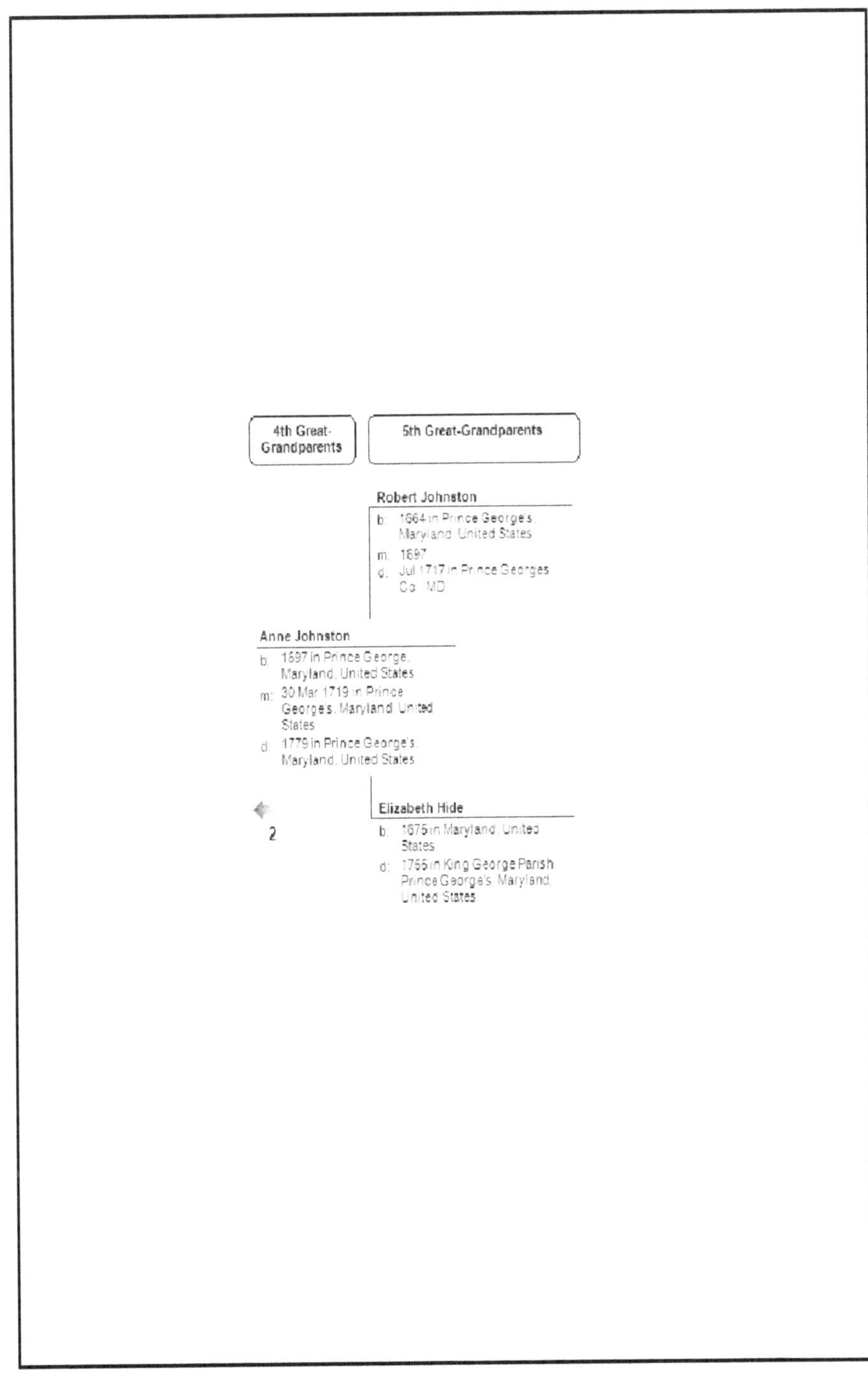

4th Great-Grandparents

5th Great-Grandparents

Robert Johnston
b: 1664 in Prince George's, Maryland, United States
m: 1697
d: Jul 1717 in Prince Georges Co., MD

Anne Johnston
b: 1697 in Prince George, Maryland, United States
m: 30 Mar 1719 in Prince Georges, Maryland, United States
d: 1779 in Prince George's, Maryland, United States

2

Elizabeth Hide
b: 1675 in Maryland, United States
d: 1765 in King George Parish, Prince George's, Maryland, United States

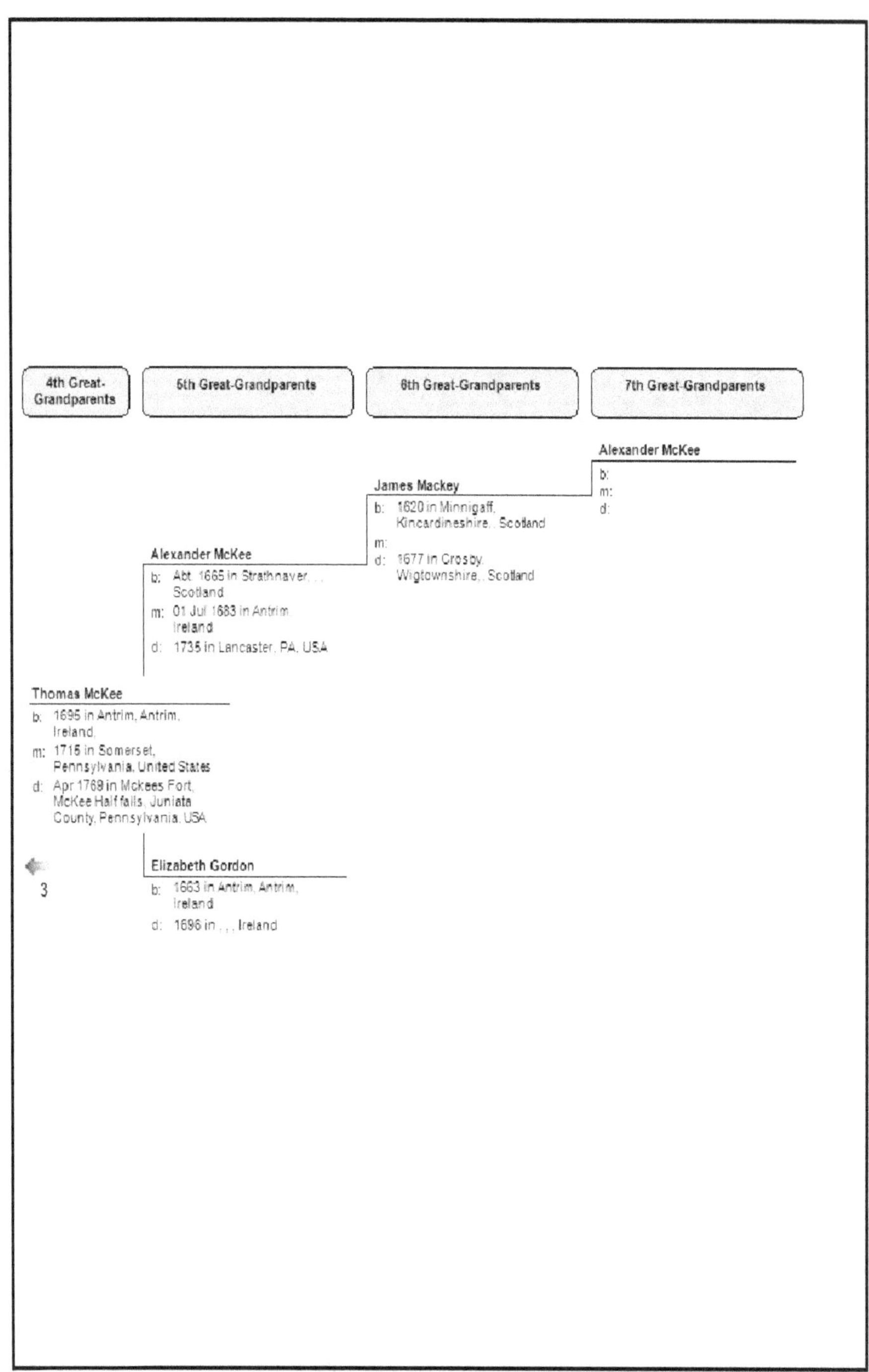

4th Great-Grandparents

5th Great-Grandparents

6th Great-Grandparents

7th Great-Grandparents

Alexander McKee
b:
m:
d:

James Mackey
b: 1620 in Minnigaff,
     Kincardineshire, . Scotland
m:
d: 1677 in Crosby,
     Wigtownshire,. Scotland

Alexander McKee
b: Abt. 1665 in Strathnaver, . .
     Scotland
m: 01 Jul 1683 in Antrim,
     Ireland
d: 1735 in Lancaster, PA, USA

Thomas McKee
b: 1695 in Antrim, Antrim,
     Ireland,
m: 1715 in Somerset,
     Pennsylvania, United States
d: Apr 1769 in Mckees Fort,
     McKee Half fails, Juniata
     County, Pennsylvania, USA

3

Elizabeth Gordon
b: 1663 in Antrim, Antrim,
     Ireland
d: 1696 in . , . Ireland

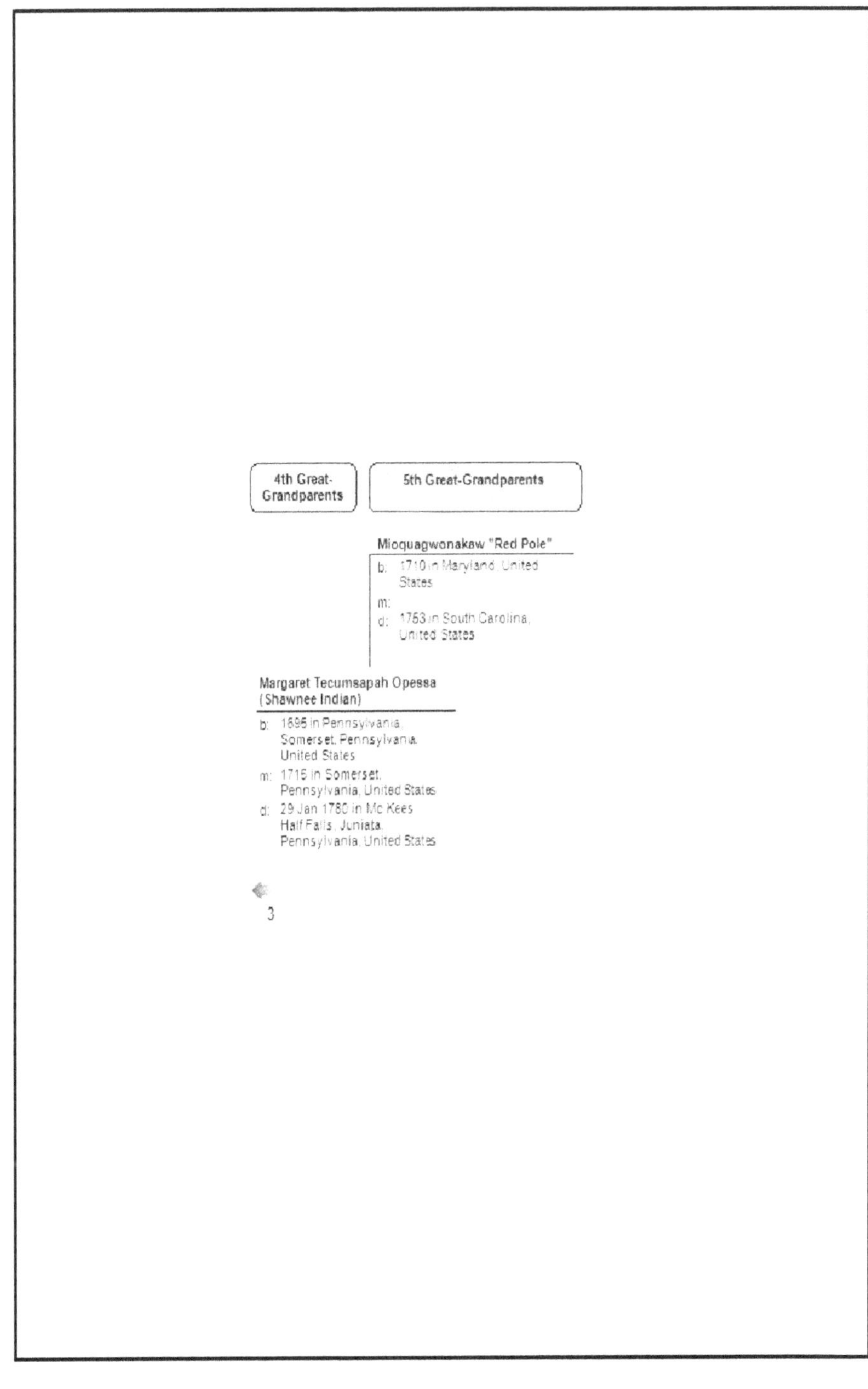

4th Great-Grandparents

5th Great-Grandparents

Mioquagwonakaw "Red Pole"
b: 1710 in Maryland, United States
m:
d: 1753 in South Carolina, United States

Margaret Tecumsapah Opessa (Shawnee Indian)
b: 1695 in Pennsylvania, Somerset, Pennsylvania, United States
m: 1715 in Somerset, Pennsylvania, United States
d: 29 Jan 1780 in Mc Kees Half Falls, Juniata, Pennsylvania, United States

3

4th Great-Grandparents

5th Great-Grandparents

6th Great-Grandparents

7th Great-Grandparents

William Thompson
b: 07 Jul 1630 in Lanark, Scotland
m: 11 Jun 1667 in Clough, Antrim, Ireland
d: 1687 in Lanark, Scotland

Hugh Thompson
b: 22 Dec 1680 in Falchfield, Lanark, Scotland
m: 04 Jun 1893 in Cough, Antrim, Ireland
d: 11 Sep 1719 in Letterkenny, Donegal, Ireland

Mary Fordyce
b: 01 Dec 1838 in Clough, Antrim, Ireland
d: , , Northern Ireland

John Thompson
b: 04 May 1695 in Letterkenny, Donegal, Ireland
m: Bet. 16 Oct 1718–1719 in Ireland
d: 1783 in Cumberland, PA

Samuel Craig
b: 1630 in Letterkenny, Donegal, Ireland
m:
d:

Margaret Craig
b: 1673
d: Letterkenny, Donegal, Ireland

Margaret Patterson
b: 1630 in Ireland
d:

Thomas Thompson
b: 06 May 1721 in Letterkenny, Donegal, Ireland
m: 11 Jun 1744 in Pennsylvania
d: 1782 in Cumberland Co. PA

3

Robert Wilson
b: 1653 in Corshill, Ayrshire, S...
m: 24 Oct 1703 in Currie, Midloth...
d: 11 Sep 1721 in Newton, Abe...

Robert Wilson
b: 1675 in Ireland
m: 1694 in Ireland
d: 1700 in Ireland

Mary Wilson
b: 02 Aug 1696 in Newton, Donegal, Ireland
d: 1724 in PA

James Gilmore
b: 1650 in Donegal, , Ireland, Scotland
m:
d:

Agnes Gilmore
b: 1675 in Newton, Donegal, Ireland
d: 1729 in , , , Ireland

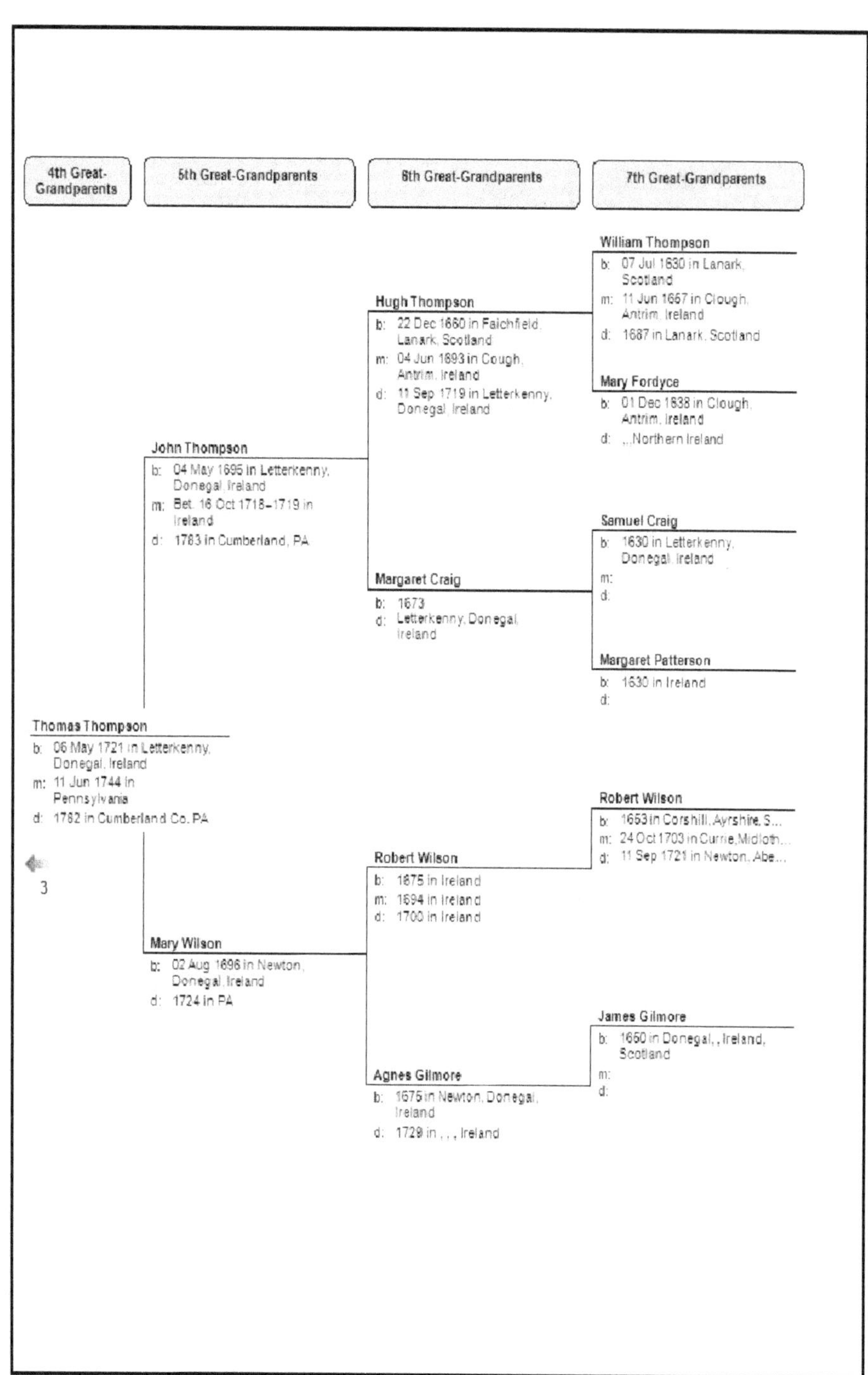

19

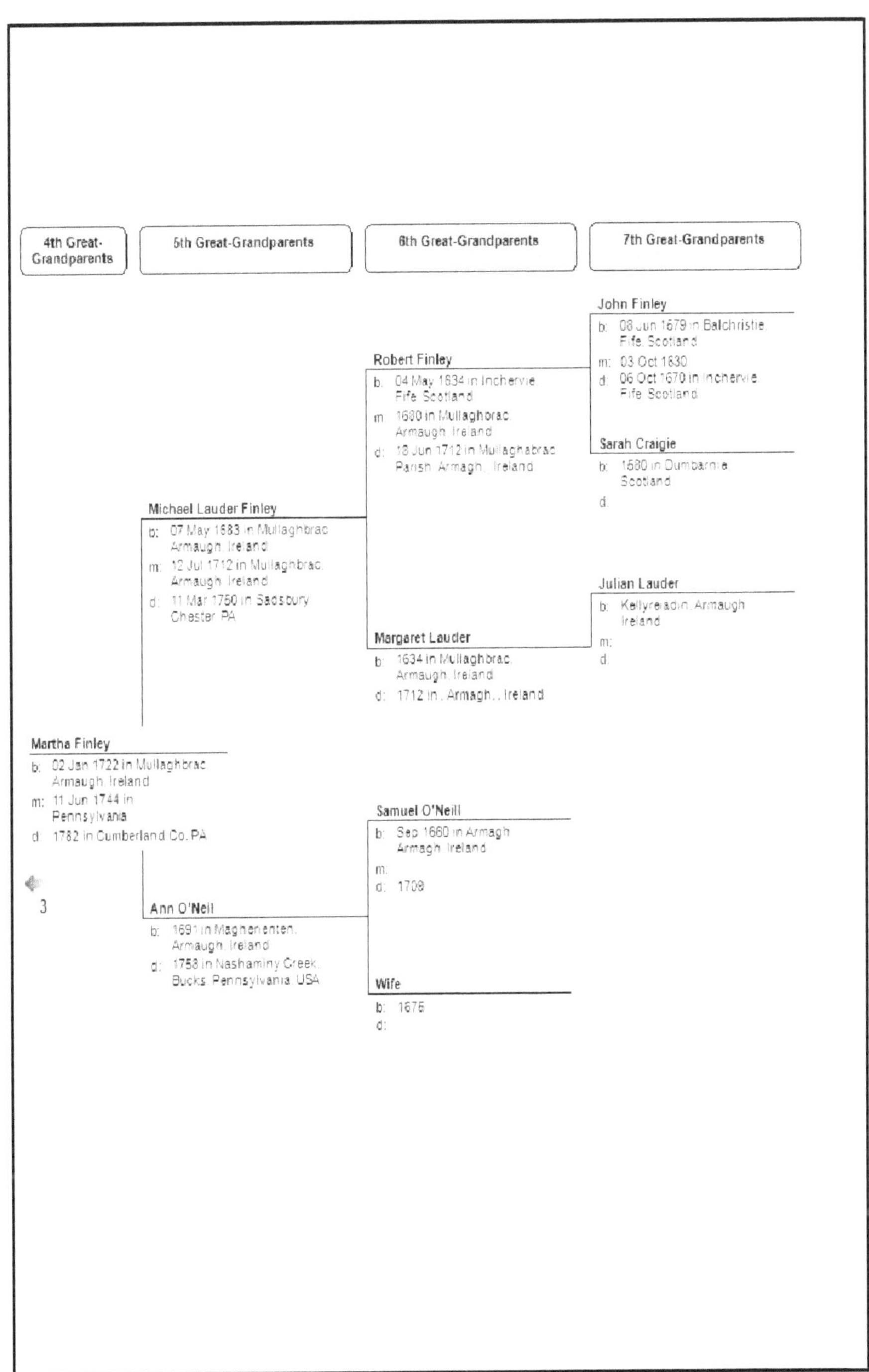

Michael Lauder Finley
- b: 07 May 1683 in Mullaghbrac, Armaugh, Ireland
- m: 12 Jul 1712 in Mullaghbrac, Armaugh, Ireland
- d: 11 Mar 1750 in Sadsbury, Chester, PA

Robert Finley
- b: 04 May 1634 in Inchervie, Fife, Scotland
- m: 1680 in Mullaghbrac, Armaugh, Ireland
- d: 18 Jun 1712 in Mullaghabrac Parish, Armagh, Ireland

John Finley
- b: 08 Jun 1679 in Balchristie, Fife, Scotland
- m: 03 Oct 1630
- d: 06 Oct 1670 in Inchervie, Fife, Scotland

Sarah Craigie
- b: 1680 in Dumbarnie, Scotland
- d:

Margaret Lauder
- b: 1634 in Mullaghbrac, Armaugh, Ireland
- d: 1712 in , Armagh., Ireland

Julian Lauder
- b: Kellyreadin, Armaugh, Ireland
- m:
- d:

Martha Finley
- b: 02 Jan 1722 in Mullaghbrac, Armaugh, Ireland
- m: 11 Jun 1744 in Pennsylvania
- d: 1782 in Cumberland Co. PA

3

Ann O'Neil
- b: 1691 in Maghenenten, Armaugh, Ireland
- d: 1758 in Nashaminy Creek, Bucks, Pennsylvania, USA

Samuel O'Neill
- b: Sep 1660 in Armagh, Armagh, Ireland
- m:
- d: 1709

Wife
- b: 1675
- d:

4th Great-Grandparents

5th Great-Grandparents

Marmaduke Watson
b: 13 Aug 1685 in Chesterfield, Burlington, New Jersey, USA
m: 27 Mar 1718 in Springfield, Burlington, New Jersey, United States
d: 24 Jul 1749 in Chesterfield, Burlington, New Jersey, USA

Aaron David Watson
b: 1720 in Chesterfield, Burlington, New Jersey, United States
m: 13 Jun 1754 in Kingwood, Hunterdon, New Jersey, USA
d: 12 Jan 1804 in Kingwood, Hunterdon, New Jersey, United States

3

Elizabeth Pancoast
b: 1697 in Mansfield, Burlington, New Jersey, USA
d: 12 Dec 1782 in Chesterfield, Burlington, New Jersey, USA

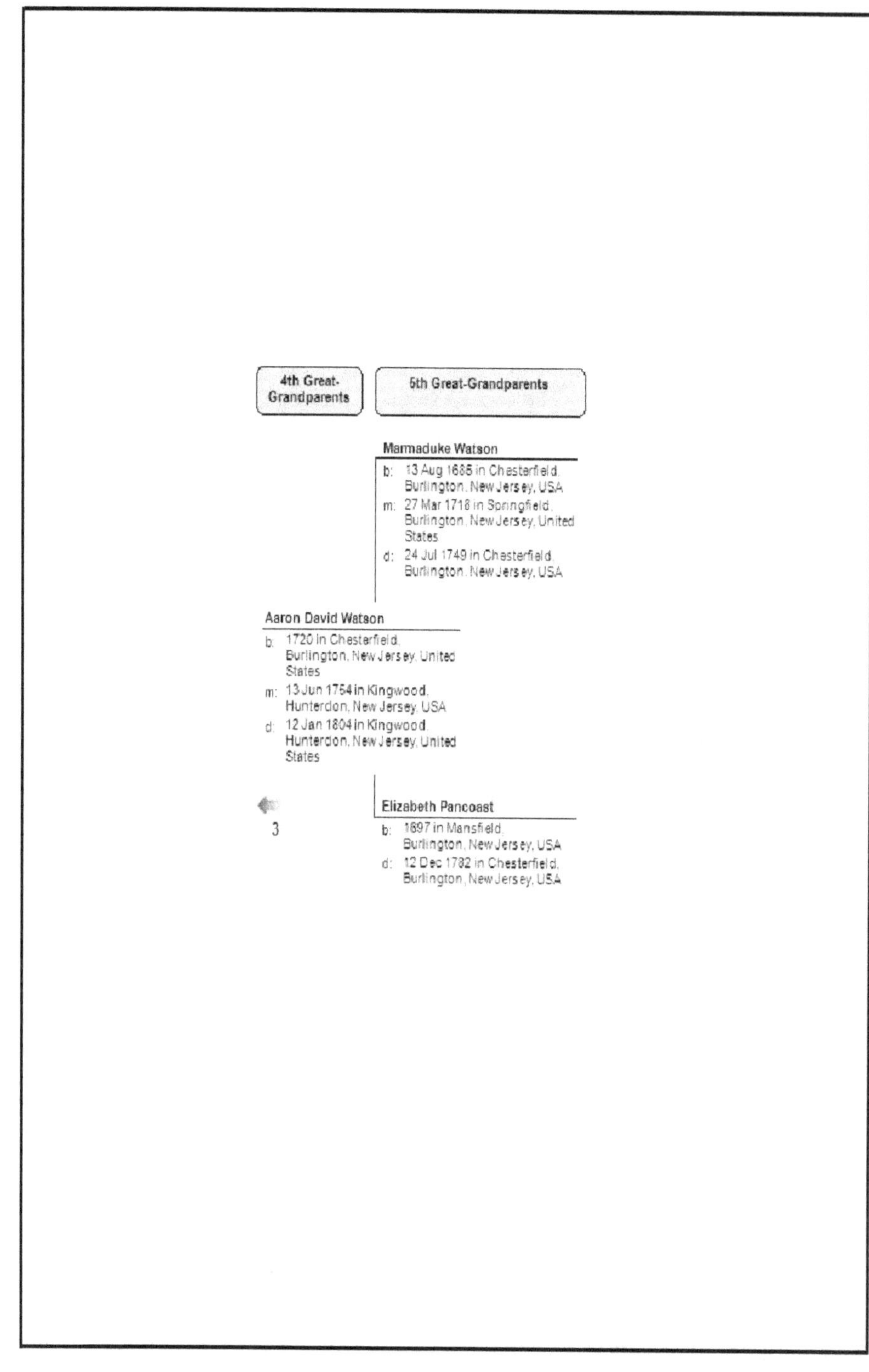

96

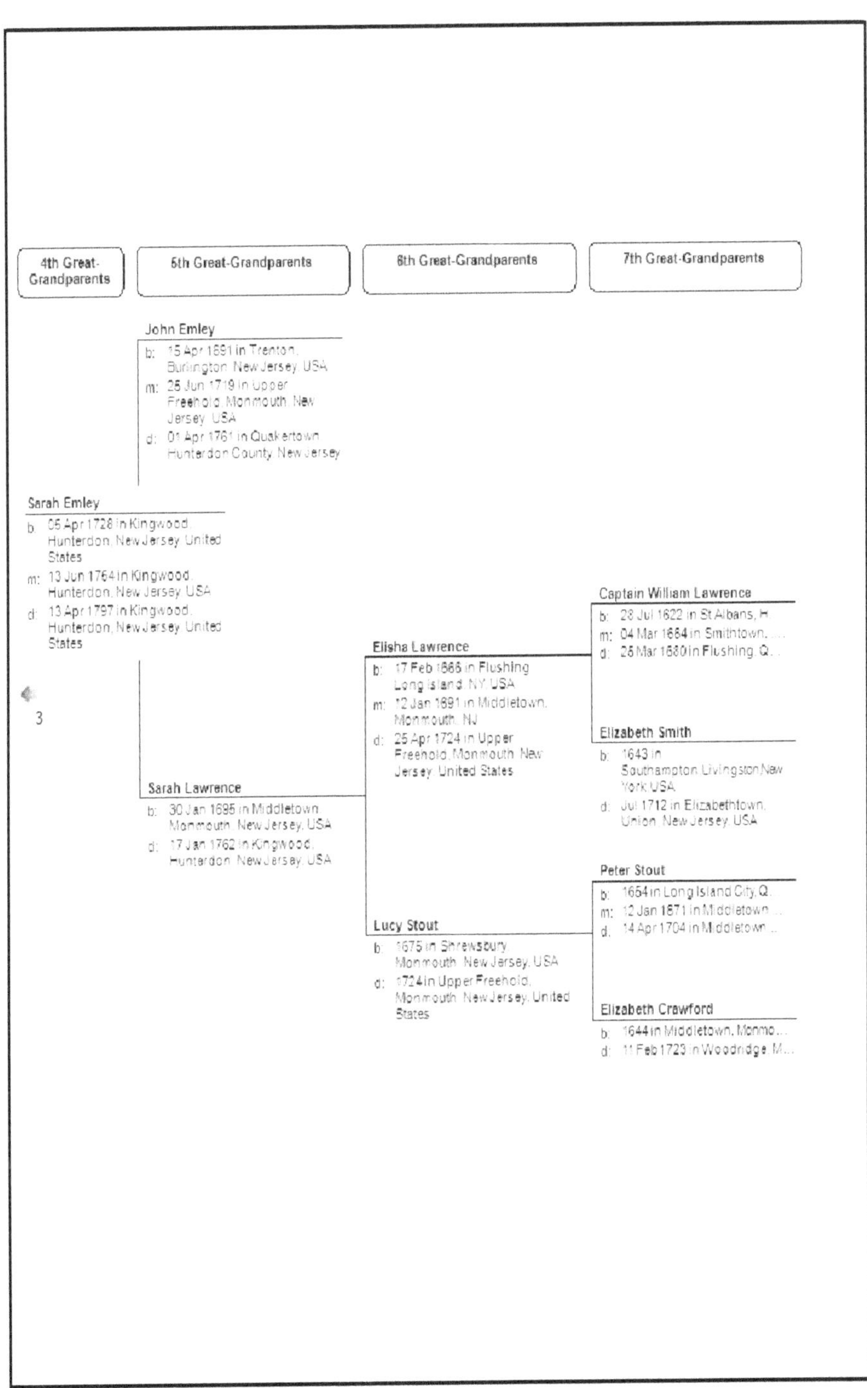

4th Great-Grandparents
5th Great-Grandparents
6th Great-Grandparents
7th Great-Grandparents

John Emley
b: 15 Apr 1691 in Trenton, Burlington, New Jersey, USA
m: 26 Jun 1719 in Upper Freehold, Monmouth, New Jersey, USA
d: 01 Apr 1761 in Quakertown, Hunterdon County, New Jersey

Sarah Emley
b: 06 Apr 1728 in Kingwood, Hunterdon, New Jersey, United States
m: 13 Jun 1764 in Kingwood, Hunterdon, New Jersey, USA
d: 13 Apr 1797 in Kingwood, Hunterdon, New Jersey, United States

3

Captain William Lawrence
b: 28 Jul 1622 in St Albans, H...
m: 04 Mar 1684 in Smithtown, ...
d: 28 Mar 1680 in Flushing, Q...

Elisha Lawrence
b: 17 Feb 1666 in Flushing, Long Island, NY, USA
m: 12 Jan 1691 in Middletown, Monmouth, NJ
d: 25 Apr 1724 in Upper Freehold, Monmouth, New Jersey, United States

Elizabeth Smith
b: 1643 in Southampton, Livingston, New York, USA
d: Jul 1712 in Elizabethtown, Union, New Jersey, USA

Sarah Lawrence
b: 30 Jan 1695 in Middletown, Monmouth, New Jersey, USA
d: 17 Jan 1762 in Kingwood, Hunterdon, New Jersey, USA

Peter Stout
b: 1664 in Long Island City, Q...
m: 12 Jan 1671 in Middletown ...
d: 14 Apr 1704 in Middletown ...

Lucy Stout
b: 1675 in Shrewsbury, Monmouth, New Jersey, USA
d: 1724 in Upper Freehold, Monmouth, New Jersey, United States

Elizabeth Crawford
b: 1644 in Middletown, Monmo...
d: 11 Feb 1723 in Woodridge, M...

4th Great-Grandparents

6th Great-Grandparents

6th Great-Grandparents

7th Great-Grandparents

Malcolm R McIntire
b: 1608 in Argyllshire, Scotland
m:
d: 1650 in Scotland

Philip Mc Intire
b: 1640 in Donegal, Ireland
m:
d: 1739 in Donegal, Ireland

Thomas Mc Intire
b: 1681 in Donegal, Ireland
m: 1701 in Donegal, Ireland
d: 1780 in Donegal, Ireland

Elizabeth McGettigan
b: 1844 in , , Donegal, Ireland
d: 1732 in , , Donegal, Ireland

Andrew McIntyre
b: 1719 in Donegal, Ireland
m: 1737
d: 24 Feb 1781 in
   Cumberland, Pennsylvania,
   United States

7

Mary Morrison
b: 1687 in Donegal, Ireland
d: 1769 in Donegal, Ireland

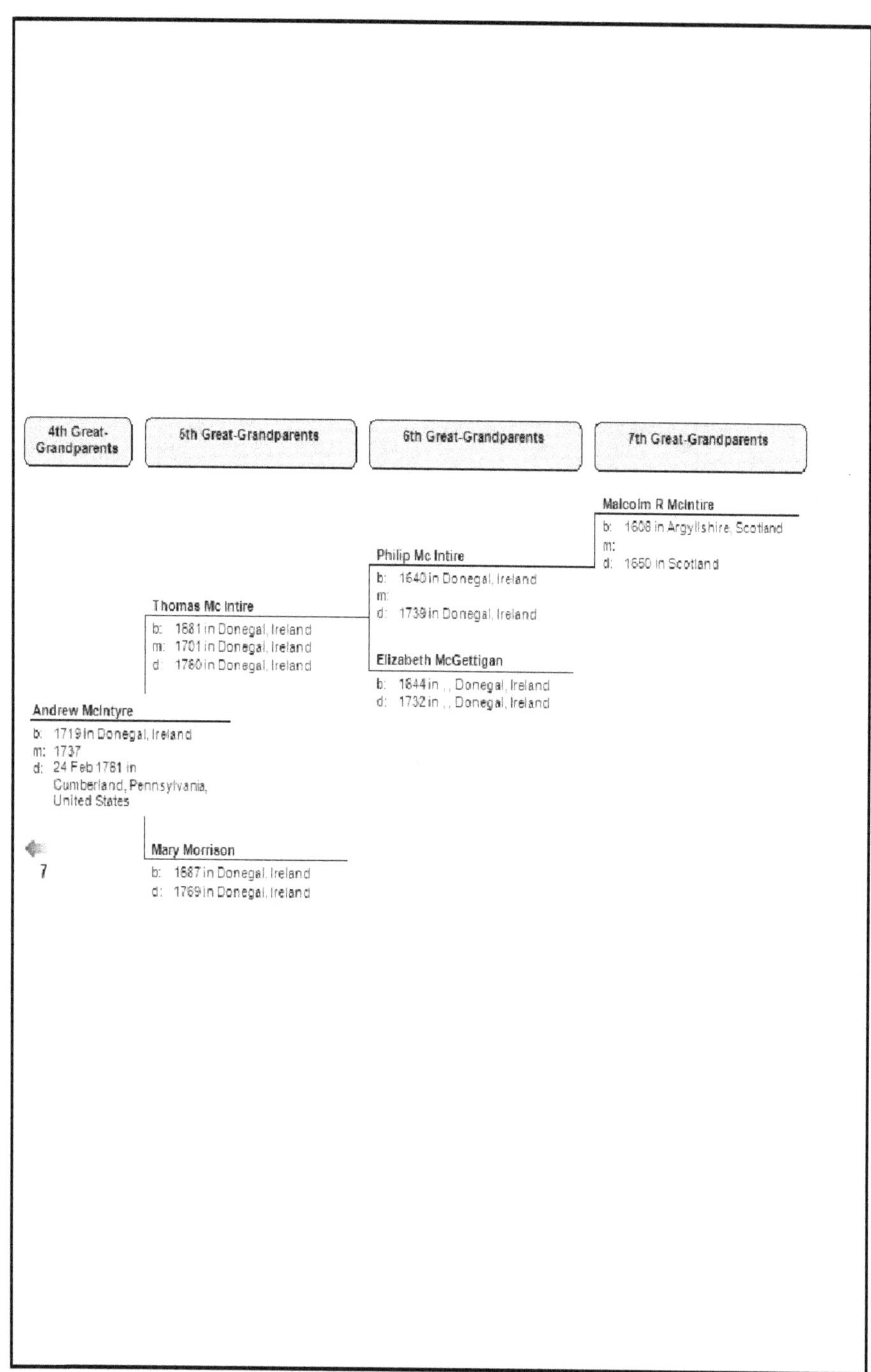

23

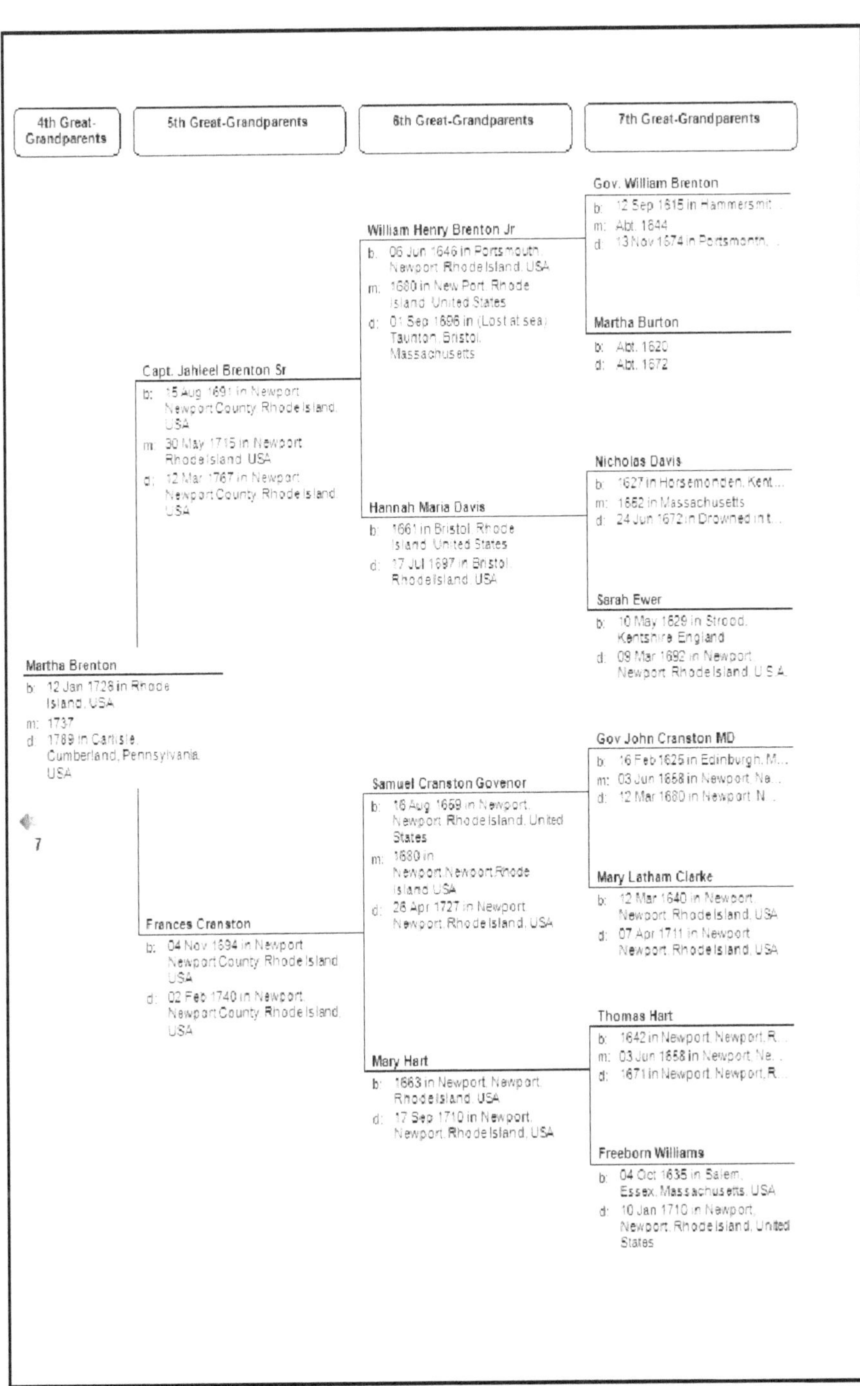

4th Great-Grandparents

5th Great-Grandparents

6th Great-Grandparents

7th Great-Grandparents

Gov. William Brenton
b: 12 Sep 1615 in Hammersmit...
m: Abt. 1644
d: 13 Nov 1674 in Portsmonth...

William Henry Brenton Jr
b: 06 Jun 1646 in Portsmouth,
Newport,Rhode Island, USA
m: 1680 in New Port, Rhode
Island, United States
d: 01 Sep 1696 in (Lost at sea)
Taunton, Bristol,
Massachusetts

Martha Burton
b: Abt. 1620
d: Abt. 1672

Capt. Jahleel Brenton Sr
b: 15 Aug 1691 in Newport,
Newport County, Rhode Island,
USA
m: 30 May 1715 in Newport,
Rhode Island, USA
d: 12 Mar 1767 in Newport,
Newport County, Rhode Island,
USA

Nicholas Davis
b: 1627 in Horsemonden, Kent...
m: 1652 in Massachusetts
d: 24 Jun 1672 in Drowned in t...

Hannah Maria Davis
b: 1661 in Bristol, Rhode
Island, United States
d: 17 JUI 1697 in Bristol,
Rhode Island, USA

Sarah Ewer
b: 10 May 1629 in Strood,
Kentshire, England
d: 09 Mar 1692 in Newport,
Newport, Rhode Island, U.S.A.

Martha Brenton
b: 12 Jan 1728 in Rhode
Island, USA
m: 1737
d: 1789 in Carlisle,
Cumberland, Pennsylvania,
USA

7

Gov John Cranston MD
b: 16 Feb 1625 in Edinburgh, M...
m: 03 Jun 1658 in Newport, Ne...
d: 12 Mar 1680 in Newport, N...

Samuel Cranston Govenor
b: 16 Aug 1669 in Newport,
Newport, Rhode Island, United
States
m: 1680 in
Newport,Newport,Rhode
Island, USA
d: 26 Apr 1727 in Newport,
Newport, Rhode Island, USA

Mary Latham Clarke
b: 12 Mar 1640 in Newport,
Newport, Rhode Island, USA
d: 07 Apr 1711 in Newport,
Newport, Rhode Island, USA

Frances Cranston
b: 04 Nov 1694 in Newport,
Newport County, Rhode Island,
USA
d: 02 Feb 1740 in Newport,
Newport County, Rhode Island,
USA

Thomas Hart
b: 1642 in Newport, Newport, R...
m: 03 Jun 1658 in Newport, Ne...
d: 1671 in Newport, Newport, R...

Mary Hart
b: 1663 in Newport, Newport,
Rhode Island, USA
d: 17 Sep 1710 in Newport,
Newport, Rhode Island, USA

Freeborn Williams
b: 04 Oct 1635 in Salem,
Essex, Massachusetts, USA
d: 10 Jan 1710 in Newport,
Newport, Rhode Island, United
States

<table><tr><td>4th Great-Grandparents</td><td>5th Great-Grandparents</td></tr></table>

Thomas Willets Sr
b: 03 May 1650 in Hempstead, Nassau, New York, USA
m: 1670 in Jericho, Nassau, New York, United States
d: 15 Jun 1714 in Islip, Suffolk, New York, United States

Thomas Willets
b: 16 May 1682 in Queens (now Nassau) County, Long Island, New York
m: 24 Dec 1706 in Westbury, Long Island, NY
d: 1772 in Pennnsylvinia or Islip, New York

7

Dinah Townsend
b: 1661 in Warwick, Kent, Rhode Island, United States
d: 18 Dec 1732 in Islip, Suffolk, New York, United States

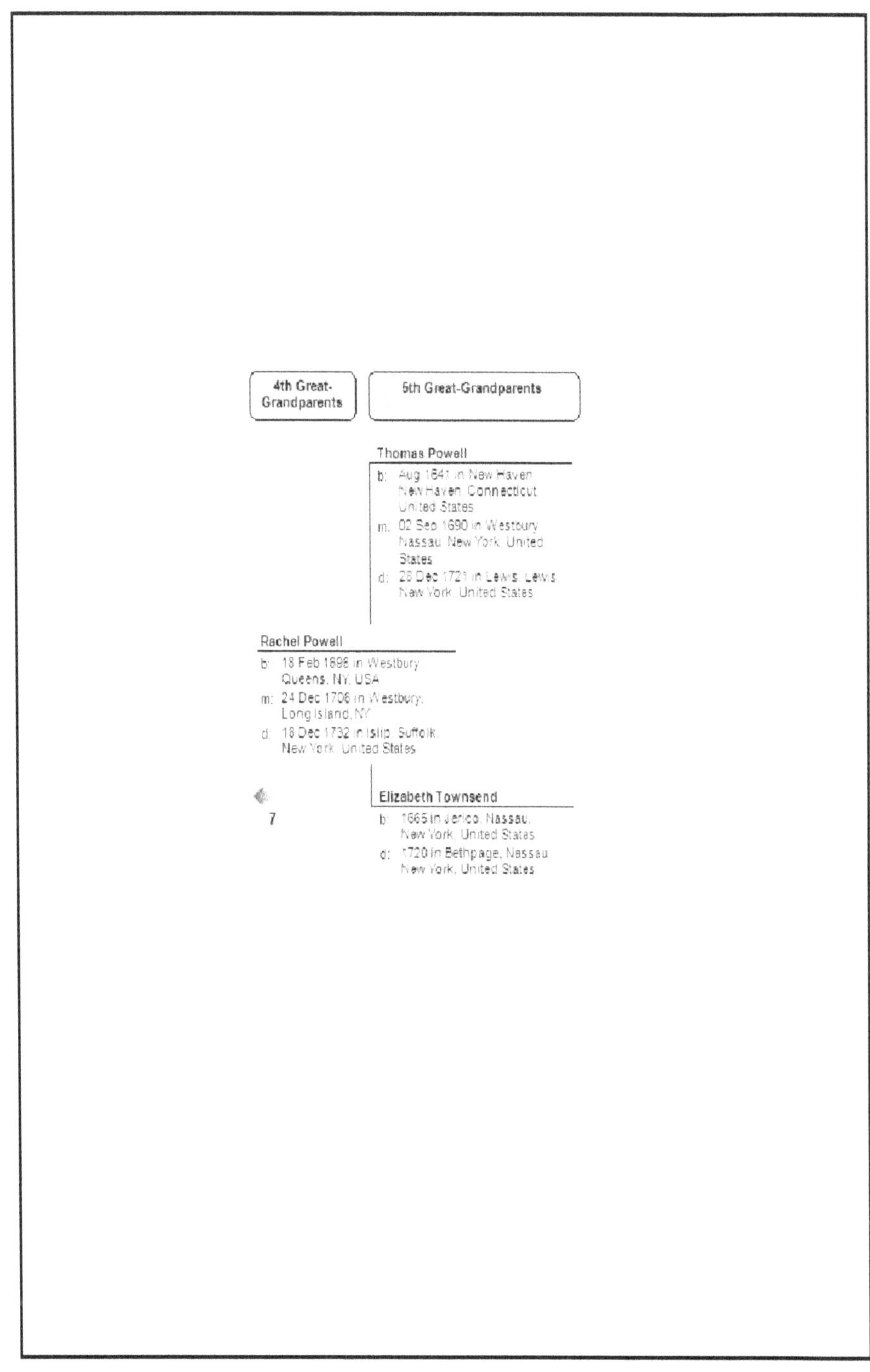

4th Great-Grandparents
5th Great-Grandparents

Thomas Powell
b: Aug 1641 in New Haven, New Haven, Connecticut, United States
m: 02 Sep 1690 in Westbury, Nassau, New York, United States
d: 28 Dec 1721 in Lewis, Lewis, New York, United States

Rachel Powell
b: 18 Feb 1698 in Westbury, Queens, NY, USA
m: 24 Dec 1706 in Westbury, Long Island, NY
d: 18 Dec 1732 in Islip, Suffolk, New York, United States

7

Elizabeth Townsend
b: 1665 in Jerico, Nassau, New York, United States
d: 1720 in Bethpage, Nassau, New York, United States

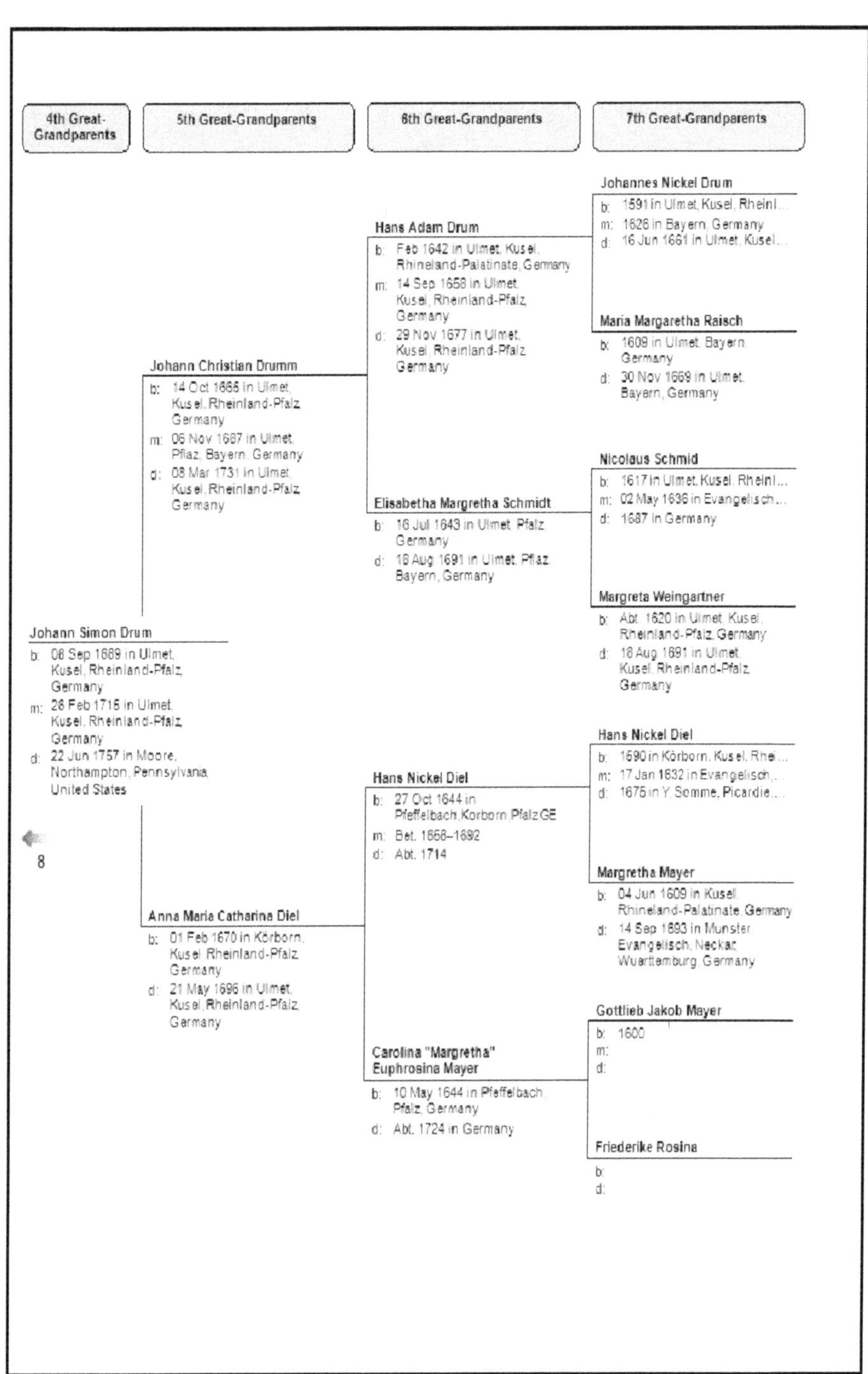

4th Great-Grandparents

5th Great-Grandparents

6th Great-Grandparents

7th Great-Grandparents

Johann Simon Drum
b: 08 Sep 1689 in Ulmet, Kusel, Rheinland-Pfalz, Germany
m: 28 Feb 1715 in Ulmet, Kusel, Rheinland-Pfalz, Germany
d: 22 Jun 1757 in Moore, Northampton, Pennsylvania, United States

8

Johann Christian Drumm
b: 14 Oct 1666 in Ulmet, Kusel, Rheinland-Pfalz, Germany
m: 06 Nov 1687 in Ulmet, Pflaz, Bayern, Germany
d: 08 Mar 1731 in Ulmet, Kusel, Rheinland-Pfalz, Germany

Anna Maria Catharina Diel
b: 01 Feb 1670 in Körborn, Kusel, Rheinland-Pfalz, Germany
d: 21 May 1696 in Ulmet, Kusel, Rheinland-Pfalz, Germany

Hans Adam Drum
b: Feb 1642 in Ulmet, Kusel, Rhineland-Palatinate, Germany
m: 14 Sep 1658 in Ulmet, Kusel, Rheinland-Pfalz, Germany
d: 29 Nov 1677 in Ulmet, Kusel, Rheinland-Pfalz, Germany

Elisabetha Margretha Schmidt
b: 16 Jul 1643 in Ulmet, Pfalz, Germany
d: 18 Aug 1691 in Ulmet, Pfalz, Bayern, Germany

Hans Nickel Diel
b: 27 Oct 1644 in Pfeffelbach, Korborn, Pfalz GE
m: Bet. 1668–1692
d: Abt. 1714

Carolina "Margretha" Euphrosina Mayer
b: 10 May 1644 in Pfeffelbach, Pfalz, Germany
d: Abt. 1724 in Germany

Johannes Nickel Drum
b: 1591 in Ulmet, Kusel, Rheinl...
m: 1626 in Bayern, Germany
d: 16 Jun 1661 in Ulmet, Kusel...

Maria Margaretha Raisch
b: 1609 in Ulmet, Bayern, Germany
d: 30 Nov 1669 in Ulmet, Bayern, Germany

Nicolaus Schmid
b: 1617 in Ulmet, Kusel, Rheinl...
m: 02 May 1636 in Evangelisch...
d: 1687 in Germany

Margreta Weingartner
b: Abt. 1620 in Ulmet, Kusel, Rheinland-Pfalz, Germany
d: 18 Aug 1691 in Ulmet, Kusel, Rheinland-Pfalz, Germany

Hans Nickel Diel
b: 1690 in Körborn, Kusel, Rhe...
m: 17 Jan 1832 in Evangelisch,...
d: 1675 in Y, Somme, Picardie...

Margretha Mayer
b: 04 Jun 1609 in Kusel, Rhineland-Palatinate, Germany
d: 14 Sep 1693 in Munster, Evangelisch, Neckar, Wuarttemburg, Germany

Gottlieb Jakob Mayer
b: 1600
m:
d:

Friederike Rosina
b:
d:

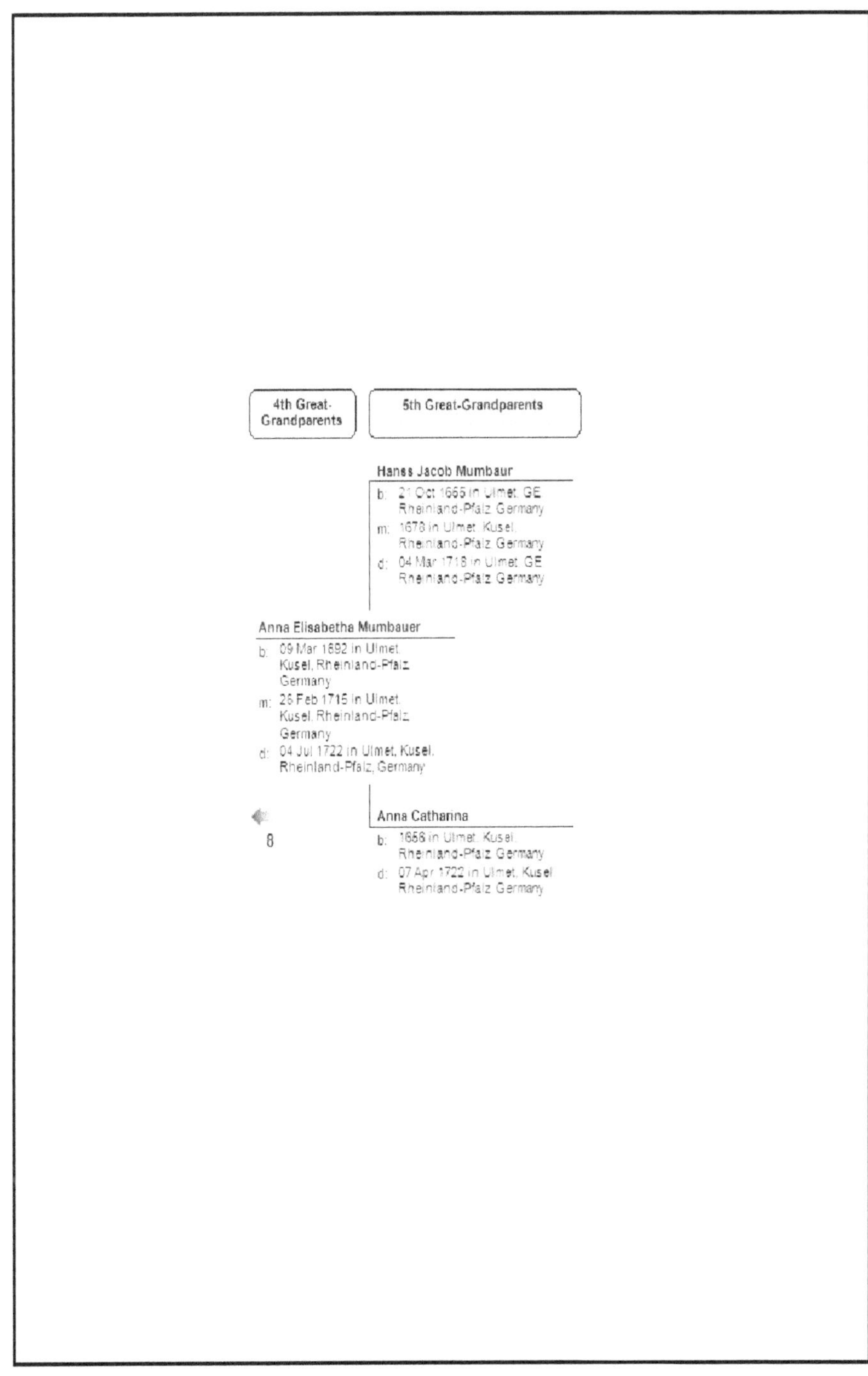

28

4th Great-Grandparents

5th Great-Grandparents

6th Great-Grandparents

Joseph Lauffer
b: 1630 in Sand, Aichach-Friedberg, Bayern, Germany
m: 18 Feb 1879
d: 03 Sep 1713 in Sand, Kusel, Rheinland-Pfalz, Germany

Joseph Lauffer
b: 18 Feb 1660 in Weisenheim am Sand, Aichach-Friedberg, Bayern, Germany
m: 18 Feb 1680 in Sand, Aichach-Friedberg, Bayern, Germany
d: 03 Sep 1713 in Weisenheim Am Sand, Bad Durkheim, Rheinland-Pfalz, Germany

Elizabeth Fischer
b: 1639 in Germany
d: 1686

Johanna Henrich Lauffer
b: 25 Mar 1683 in Weisenheim am Sand, Bad Durkheim, Rheinland-Pfalz, Germany
m: 11 Jul 1708 in Weisenheim (Am Sand), Bayern, Germany
d: 02 Mar 1729 in Weisenheim am Sand, Bad Durkheim, Rheinland-Pfalz, Germany

8

Ludwig Fischer
b: 1630 in Bad Homburg, Hochtaunuskreis, Hessen, Germany
m:
d: 1669 in Germany

Sophia Elisabetha Fischer
b: 1661 in Rheinbaiern, Germany
d: 1686 in Pittsburgh, Allegheny, Pennsylvania, United States

Catherine
b: 1638 in Hesse, Germany
d: Aft. 1661 in Rheinbaiern, Germany

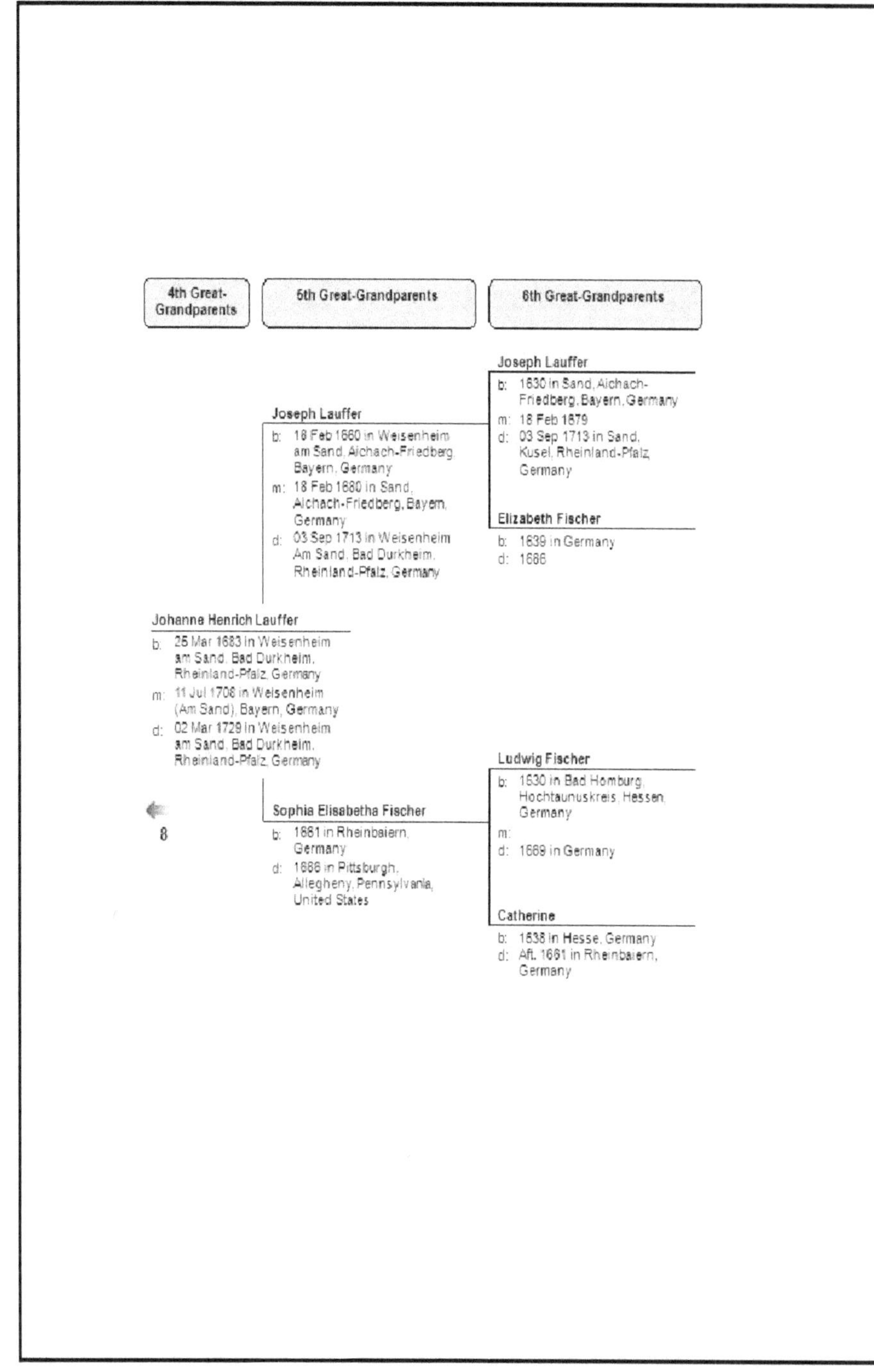

29

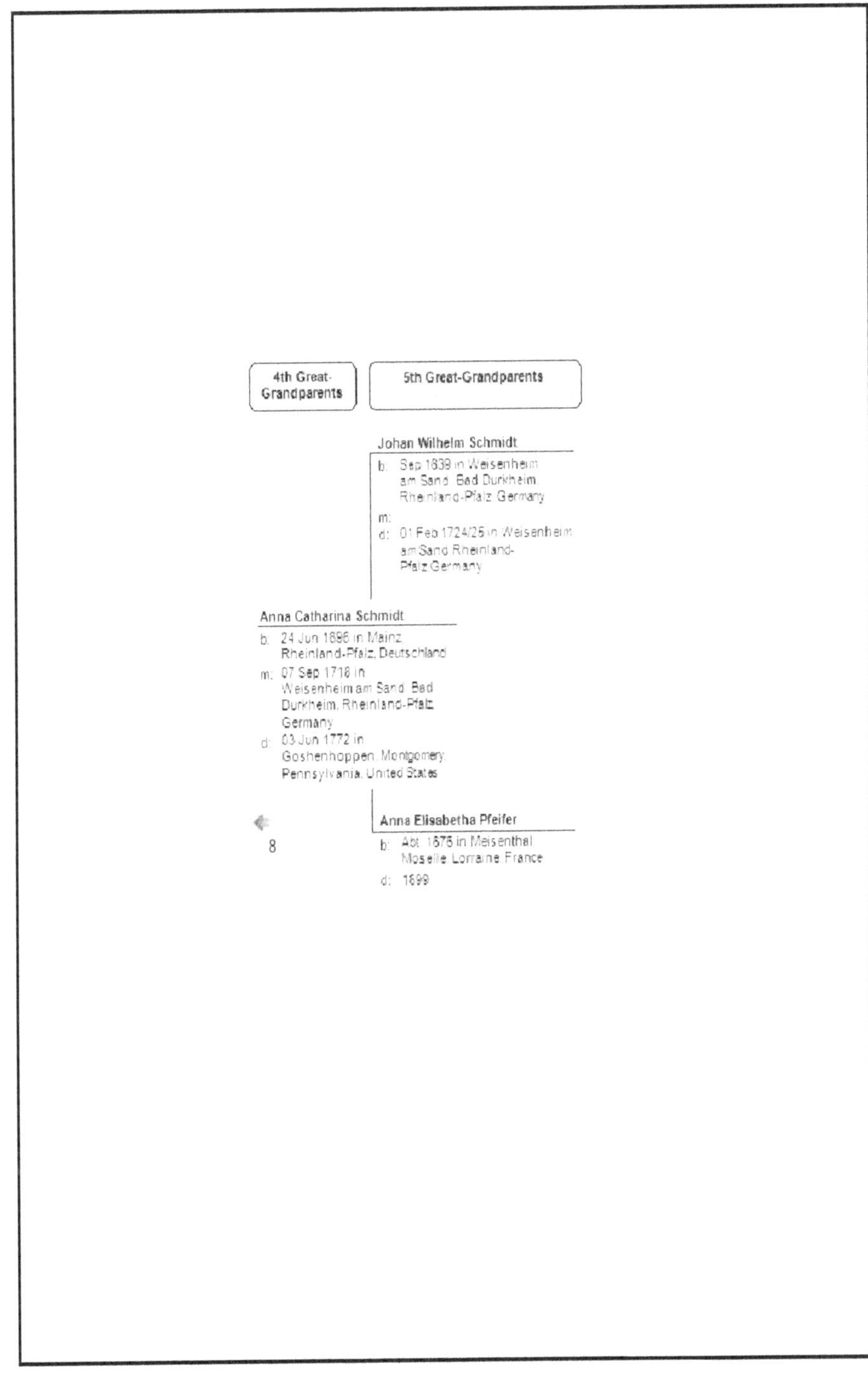

105

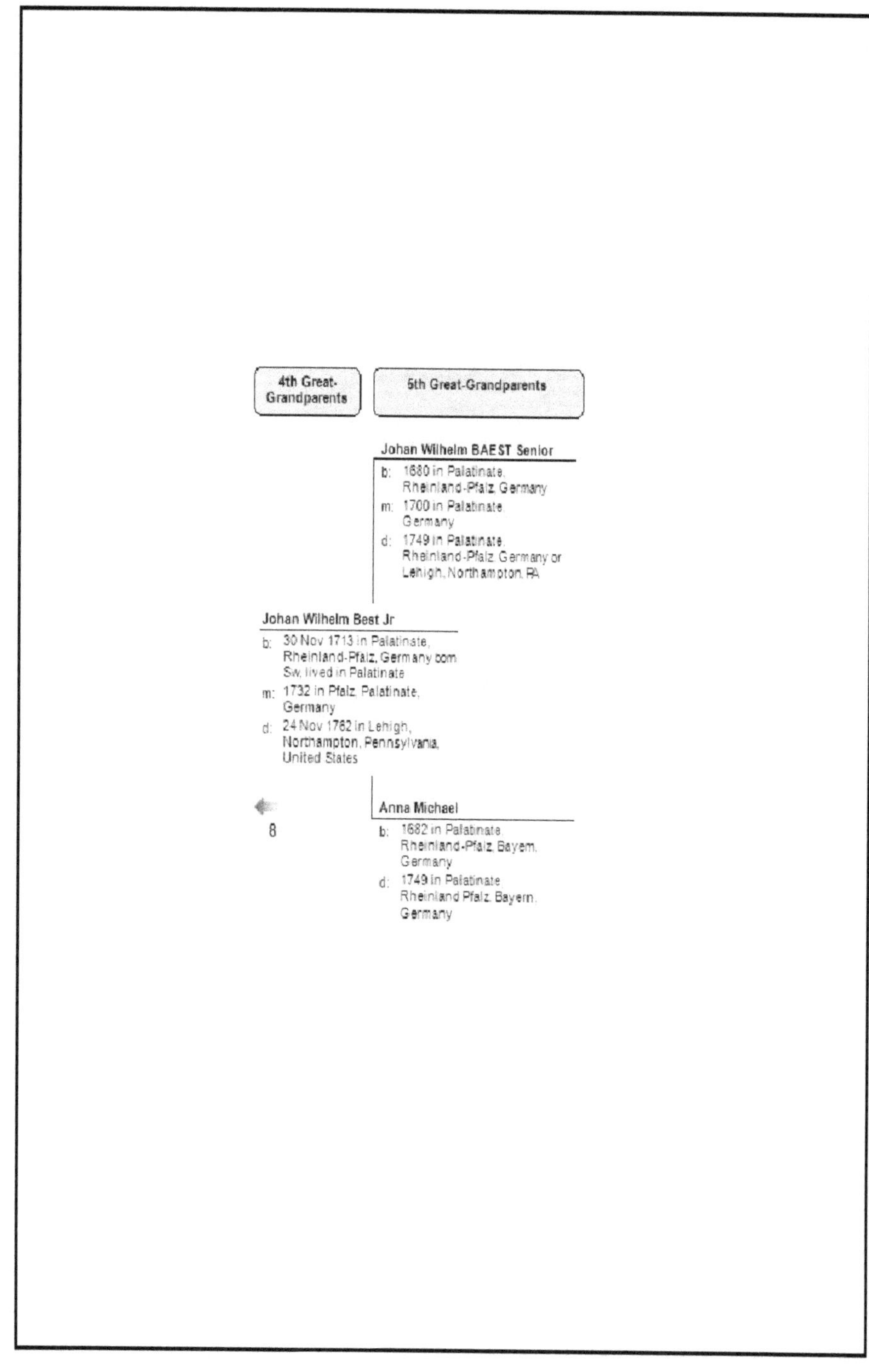

4th Great-Grandparents

5th Great-Grandparents

Johan Wilhelm BAEST Senior
b: 1680 in Palatinate,
    Rheinland-Pfalz Germany
m: 1700 in Palatinate
    Germany
d: 1749 in Palatinate,
    Rheinland-Pfalz Germany or
    Lehigh, Northampton, PA

Johan Wilhelm Best Jr
b: 30 Nov 1713 in Palatinate,
    Rheinland-Pfalz, Germany com
    Sw. lived in Palatinate
m: 1732 in Pfalz, Palatinate,
    Germany
d: 24 Nov 1762 in Lehigh,
    Northampton, Pennsylvania,
    United States

8

Anna Michael
b: 1682 in Palatinate
    Rheinland-Pfalz Bayern,
    Germany
d: 1749 in Palatinate
    Rheinland Pfalz Bayern,
    Germany

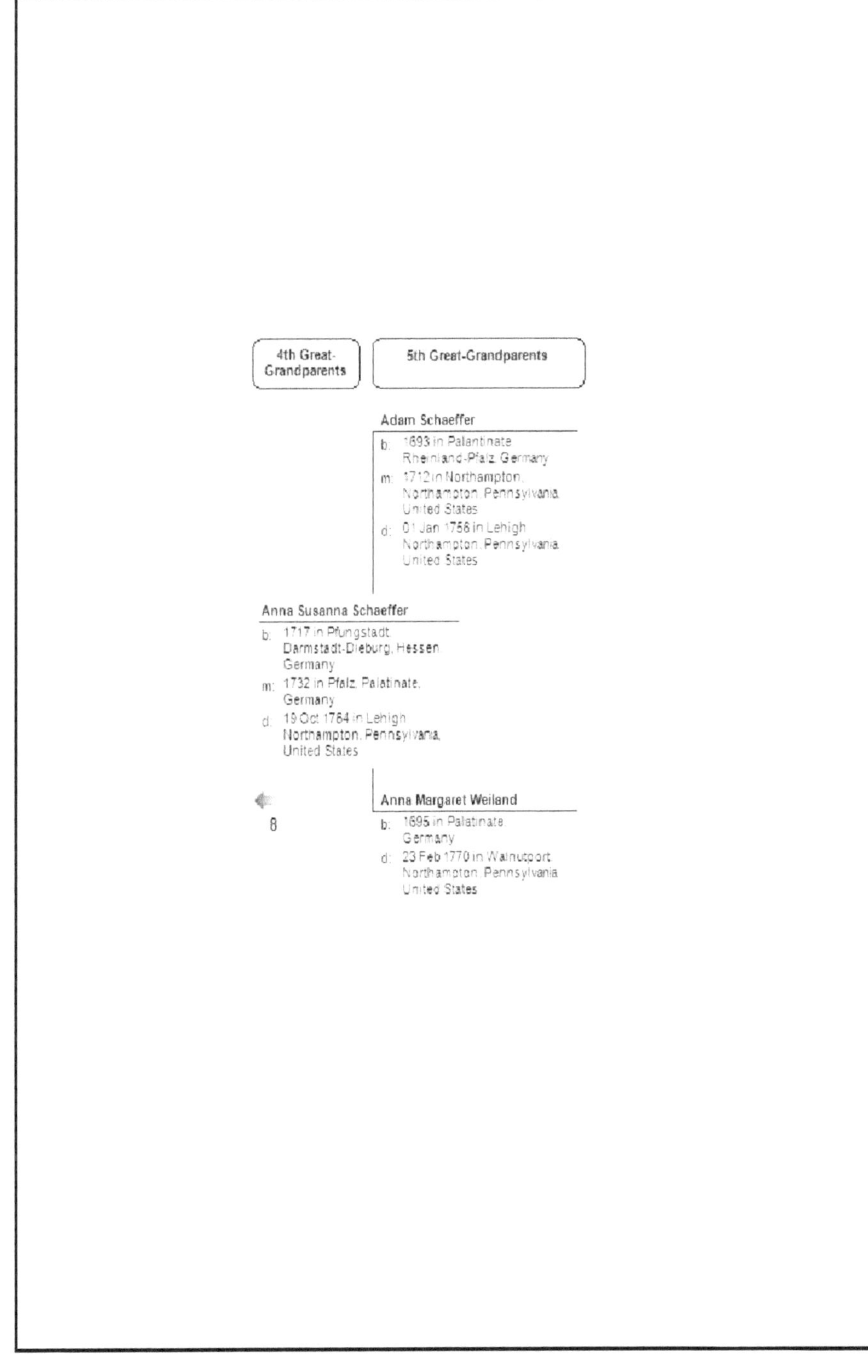
4th Great-Grandparents

5th Great-Grandparents

Adam Schaeffer
b: 1693 in Palantinate,
Rheinland-Pfalz, Germany
m: 1712 in Northampton,
Northampton, Pennsylvania,
United States
d: 01 Jan 1758 in Lehigh,
Northampton, Pennsylvania,
United States

Anna Susanna Schaeffer
b: 1717 in Pfungstadt,
Darmstadt-Dieburg, Hessen,
Germany
m: 1732 in Pfalz, Palatinate,
Germany
d: 19 Oct 1784 in Lehigh,
Northampton, Pennsylvania,
United States

8

Anna Margaret Weiland
b: 1695 in Palatinate,
Germany
d: 23 Feb 1770 in Walnutport,
Northampton, Pennsylvania,
United States

A retired Jr.-Sr. High health and physical ed teacher from Titusville, Pennsylvania, Marti Bennett first became interested in genetic health when her mother was diagnosed with Parkinson's. The family health research quickly turned into a hobby with a greater appreciation for history. Inspired by the TV series, "Who Do You Think You Are?" Marti's research branched out to include historical events. Fortunately, there are a multitude of Internet sites for amateur genealogists, plus the long Pennsylvania winters offer ample time for research.